SUDDEN EDEN

Illuminations: A Series on American Poetics
Series Editor, Jon Thompson

Illuminations focuses on the poetics and poetic practices of the contemporary moment in the USA. The series is particularly keen to promote a set of reflective works that include, but go beyond, traditional academic prose, so we take Walter Benjamin's rich, poetic essays published under the title of *Illuminations* as an example of the kind of approach we most value. Collectively, the titles published in this series aim to engage various audiences in a dialogue that will reimagine the field of contemporary American poetics. For more about the series, please visit its website at parlorpress.com/illuminations.

Books in the Series

Vestiges: Notes, Responses, and Essays 1988–2018 by Eric Pankey (2019)
Sudden Eden by Donald Revell (2019)
Prose Poetry and the City by Donna Stonecipher (2018)

SUDDEN EDEN

ESSAYS

Donald Revell

Parlor Press
Anderson, South Carolina
www.parlorpress.com

Parlor Press LLC, Anderson, South Carolina, USA
© 2019 by Parlor Press
Printed in the United States of America on acid-free paper.
   S A N: 2 5 4 - 8 8 7 9

    Library of Congress Cataloging-in-Publication Data on File

Illuminations: A Series on American Poetics
Series Editor: Jon Thompson

Cover art: "Early Morning, Tarpon Springs" by George Inness,
   1892. Edward B. Butler Collection, Art Instuted of Chicago. Used
   by permission.
Interior and cover design: David Blakesley
Copyeditor: Jared Jameson

Parlor Press, LLC is an independent publisher of scholarly and trade
titles in print and multimedia formats. This book is available in paper,
cloth and eBook formats from Parlor Press on the World Wide Web at
http://www.parlorpress.com or through online and brick-and-mortar
bookstores. For submission information or to find out about Parlor Press
publications, write to Parlor Press, 3015 Brackenberry Drive, Anderson,
South Carolina, 29621, or email editor@parlorpress.com.

Contents

Acknowledgments

The author wishes to thank the editors of the following publications for offering these essays their original appearance in print:

American Letters & Commentary
American Poet
The American Poetry Review
The Ben Jonson Journal
Chicago Review
Denver Quarterly
Omnidawn
Omniverse
Pequod
Poetry

In Memory of Burton Feldman

SUDDEN EDEN

Wine Instead of Whiskey for a While

Another world? I can only think of Paradise, the one place I entirely remember, not as it was, but as it IS. (Surely it's the flawless imperfection of that rhyme—Para*dise* and *Is*—that explains so much for me: hummingbirds; clematis; the Rip van Winkle Bridge; Kerouac's drinking to the daytime reruns, *The Beverly Hillbillies*; and how, standing in the shower five minutes ago, I thought of my mother and of her soothing my father with baby powder while he died.)

There's nothing else to think of. Paradise.

The first time I remember being there, I was five years old and my father was driving. I've written about it.

> When I was a boy, my father drove us once
> very fast along a road deep in a woodland.
> The leaves on the trees turned into mirrors
> signaling with bright lights frantically.
> They said it was the end of the world and to go faster.
> ("How Passion Comes to Matter" 1-5)

We were in the Catskills. Suddenly, the road ahead and the woods around us turned a brilliantly bright, but not blinding, pure white. My father kept driving. There were no cars but ours. After a while, my mother and sister and I began to chatter, at first frantically but then delightedly, about how beautiful the white forest and all the white leaves (this was middle July) and pine needles seemed in the perfect sunlight. It was clear to us all, though nobody said so, that we had somehow died and were motoring through Heaven now. Having no reason to slow down, my father drove faster and faster. After a few more minutes, the trees were just as suddenly green again and the two-lane blacktop asphalt black. We got home fine and had our supper.

I mean to find that stretch of road again. It would make things easy and save me a fortune in books and alcohol. All through my childhood, I looked for some precipice or hilltop from which I'd see the road and leap down into it. ["Like swimmers into cleanness leaping" ("Peace" 4), as Rupert Brooke wrote one time—but I get ahead of myself, and of him.] No such luck. Not yet. But in the meantime, poetry, like the glitter of sunshine in a wine-cup on summer mornings, keeps me hopeful. I wasn't and I am not dreaming. Paradise isn't make-believe. I remember being so excited when, near the end of high school, I first read Rupert Brooke's "Dining Room Tea." Here are the first four stanzas:

> When you were there, and you, and you,
> Happiness crowned the night; I too
> Laughing and looking, one of all,
> I watched the quivering lamplight fall
> On plate and flowers and pouring tea
> And cup and cloth; and they and we
> Flung all the dancing moments by
> With jest and glitter. Lip and eye
> Flashed on the glory, shone and cried,
> Improvident, unmemoried;
> And fitfully and like a flame
> The light of laughter went and came.
> Proud in their careless transience moved
> The changing faces that I loved.
>
> Till suddenly, and otherwhence,
> I looked upon your innocence.
> For lifted clear and still and strange
> From the dark woven flow of change
> Under a vast and starless sky
> I saw the immortal moment lie.

One instant I, an instant, knew
As God knows all. And it and you

I, above Time, oh, blind! could see
In witless immortality.
I saw the marble cup; the tea,
Hung on the air, an amber stream;
I saw the fire's unglittering gleam,
The painted flame, the frozen smoke.
No more the flooding lamplight broke
On flying eyes and lips and hair;
But lay, but slept unbroken there,
On stiller flesh, and body breathless,
And lips and laughter stayed and deathless,
And words on which no silence grew.
Light was more alive than you.

For suddenly, and otherwhence,
I looked on your magnificence.
I saw the stillness and the light,
And you, august, immortal, white,
Holy and strange; and every glint
Posture and jest and thought and tint
Freed from the mask of transiency,
Triumphant in eternity,
Immote, immortal.

Like me, Rupert Brooke had been to Paradise *in company*.
Of course, being in Europe, his Paradise was vertical, neo-Pla-
tonic if you will, and not a horizontal stretch of Catskills asphalt. And having been born in the nineteenth century, *he* saw
a stillness where I'd seen speed. "Shall we &/why not, buy a
goddamn big car" . . . ("I Know a Man" 8-9). Creeley's great
poem remains a frantic tender Paradise too. What mattered
then, at the end of high school, and what matters still unstill to
me is the co-*incidence* of a co-*extensive* Paradise: momentary but
continuous; intermittent but eternal, at least so far. And who
knows? Given the right poem or precipice (a great poem *is* a
precipice), Paradise might become full-time.

In the meantime, there is the search for means of coping with Paradisiac nostalgia. How does one go forward with a memory of Paradise driving?

> Le Paradis n'est pas artificiel
> > but is jagged
> For a flash,
> > for an hour.
> Then agony,
> > then an hour,
> > > then agony . . .
> > > > (Pound, "Canto XCII" 66-72)

The intervals of Paradise—do they exalt or agonize? Does an absolute certainty of the reality of Paradise make our daily rigmaroles of imbecility and rapacity, ache and anomie more or less possible to bear? Always, it would seem, there is a choice to make—between a wild impatience and a sometimes even wilder willingness to bide. Less than a week before he died, Dylan Thomas gave apt, anguished expression to his own particular wilderness limit and love. Confiding to a friend, he said—"I want to go to the Garden of Eden . . . to die . . ." (Read 173).

No poet of our time had a more vivid or vivifying conviction of Eden's continuing access than did Dylan Thomas.

> And then to awake, and the farm, like a wanderer white
> With the dew, come back, the cock on his shoulder: it
> > was all
> > > Shining, it was Adam and maiden,
> > > > The sky gathered again
> > > And the sun grew round that very day.
> > > > ("Fern Hill" 28-32)

Yet clearly, evidence of Paradise may sustain a life even as it drives it wildly to an end. In "The First Century," Thomas Traherne avowed "Your enjoyment of the World is never right, till every Morning you awake in Heaven." It is that one word "every" that drives me crazy, just as I'm certain it drove Dylan

Thomas to those eighteen straight whiskies that were the death of him. Having, alive, with eyes wide open, witnessed the renovation by Paradise of common Day one day, or even often, what about another? What happens when I wake wrong and do not enjoy the world aright? There is always the great escape, the wild impatience. Too, there is one or another lesser precipice, a little while longer in the wilderness of poems, of pictures, of baseball with the kids, white wine in the morning instead of whiskey. My life is mostly a little wild abiding. One time last year I was at loose ends and lonely in Chicago. I'd read my poems to some lovely people and had another day to spend before I could go home. I went to the Art Institute where I saw so many heavenly pictures (one of them a Catskills landscape, so very, very close), it almost made me frantic. And then I turned a corner into a small room, one entire wall of which was taken up by an enormous Vuillard—*Foliage—Oak Tree & Fruit Seller.* In the lower left-hand corner of the canvas, a little girl bends down through blue-green shade to touch a white kitten. I sat on the floor in front of the picture, and I watched the kitten and the girl for a whole half hour. A lesser precipice, such as Hart Crane showed, a "kitten in the wilderness" ("Chaplinesque" 23).

I know a Paradise when I see one, because I've seen one. The trick is now to see another till I see One again.

1

The Apostasy of Here and Now:
Easters with Traherne

During Easter Week of 2001, I wrote a poem (later collected in *My Mojave*) entitled "For Thomas Traherne."

The ground is tender with cold rain
Far and equally
Our coastlines grow younger
With tides
Beautiful winter
Not becoming spring today and not tomorrow
Has time to stay

Easter will be very late this year
Thirty years ago
I saw my church
All flowery
And snow
Melting in the hair of the procession
As tender as today

A sight above all festivals or praise
Is earth everywhere
And all things here
Becoming younger
Facing change
In the dark weather now like winter
Candling underground as rain.

The poem was written by way of thanks to that poet who, more than any other, convinces me always that resurrection (and along with resurrection, every transformation I understand as the experience of poetry) is a current event. At Easter, the distance between past and present disappears, and there is only a threshold, awesome but tender, singular but eternal. The crossing is uncertain, but irresistible, and thus leads on to a certainty without end. Every Easter is an original: in snowfall, in sunshine filtered through the new green leaves, in youth, in middle age. I was given this poem in the form of an expansive single moment, thirty years long and more. Each detail simply took its proper place in a capacious Now. My faith in such a form was given to me by Traherne.

> His name is NOW, His nature is forever.
> None can His creatures from their maker sever.
> ("The Anticipation," 26–27)

All Easters are one and the same because, if they have any reality at all, they are the product not of dogma, culture, or festival habit, but rather of immediate experience. Resurrection has to *happen*. Naturally, the memory of Easters past comes forward when it does. This being the case, each and every detail of the experience takes its place in and furnishes its part unto the event. Flowers, coastlines, rain, snow, and candles all belong together, no matter what the year of their foregrounding. The experience of Easter, indeed the cumulative experience of divinity (which for Traherne is *every* experience), is a *sensation*.

> For sight inherits beauty, hearing sounds,
>   The nostril sweet perfumes,
>   All tastes have hidden rooms
> Within the tongue; and feeling feeling wounds
>   With pleasure and delight, but I
> Forgot the rest, and was all sight or eye.
>   Unbodied and devoid of care,
> Just as in Heaven the holy angels are.
>   For simple sense
> Is lord of all created excellence.
>   ("The Preparative," 31–40)

The opened eye inherits Heaven effortlessly. And every detail available to the sense of sight becomes an unassertive but indispensable agent of that event. In this passage, Traherne teaches me how to write devotion by simply devoting poems to sense. We access sensation by grace of the lordly senses. If anything comes to mind, it comes through them and is therefore current. Resurrection is immediately available. Only inattention can interrupt the prolific and ongoing miracle. Now, I would like to describe just how the poetry of Thomas Traherne and its profusive immediacies came to shape my own practice and, in truth, my best understanding of what a poet is and ought happily to be.

Chance, haphazard, and neglect combined to make Thomas Traherne the one great seventeenth-century poet who is, in every sense of influence and illumination, contemporary. In his very fact, he both embodies and reconciles the paradox that gave me the poem I wrote for him. Three hundred years remote and more, the body of his work remains very recent news, portions of it coming to light as late as 1982. To read him is to spend an Easter in Eden. And then another. And then another after that—Easters always original and always one and the same. Each is forever prefatory, a threshold where attention alone determines the meaning of each passage. Reading Traherne makes a virtue of transgression because it's Eden in every direction and every single detail. The first and second Adams meet at every crossing point, most especially where light transpires to the eye.

> All bliss
> Consists in this,
> To do as Adam did . . .
> (Traherne, "The Apostasy," 37–39)

Here is an inexhaustible permission for any poet writing now. By unconfining Eden in both space and time, Traherne makes the event of reading him into what, to borrow words from Robert Duncan, becomes "a place of first permission" ("Often I am Permitted to Return to a Meadow" 22). A poet can use Traherne, because in his poems everything that comes to light comes not at second hand, but ready-to-hand. His vision is new, no matter that a portion of this newness results from accidents of literary history, and only new visions are immediately of use. Poetry requires a new Heaven and new Earth in every word, and these Traherne joyfully, and with almost no apparent effort, abundantly provides.

> No empty space; it is all full of sight,
>> All soul and life, an eye most bright,
>>> All light and love;
> Which doth at once all things possess and give,
> Heaven and earth, and all that therein live;
>> It rests at quiet, and doth move;
>> Eternal is, yet time includes;
>>> A scene above
>>> All interludes.
>>>> ("Felicity," 19–27)

I spoke of my own poem as structured by the form of one single, expansive moment, an Easter of sorts. Here, in "Felicity," we find both the physics and the metaphysics of that moment. (In Traherne, physics and metaphysics are inextricably intertwined.) Contraries are ever so much more than reconciled. They are wed. Heaven and earth, motion and rest, eternity and time embrace in Traherne's capacious "scene / Above all interludes." And what fills the scene to overflowing is not first phenomenal but, rather, perceptual: the scene is filled by "sight." Thus does any distinction between sight and Vision disappear into a current event. And the event, being "above all interludes," cannot be interrupted or delayed. This is the news that every poet needs. The opened eye inherits Heaven effortlessly.

The release I experienced (the theme of Easter hymns is always liberation) upon coming to the poems of Thomas Traherne consisted of finding everything I had thus far loved about poetry and poets suddenly available, immediately and intimately. All my first figures, my sponsors in eternity if you will, found a further and more entire original in the son of a Hereford shoemaker and his unequivocal exaltation. My first poet, Blake, whom I found in a Bronx bookstore in the pretty green

Avon edition, circa 1969, turned out certainly to be an ephebe, albeit unknowingly, of Traherne. The passage from "Felicity" cited above, is it not the perfect articulation, in advance, of Blake's "Without contraries is no progression?" ("The Marriage of Heaven and Hell" 28) Walking the Grand Concourse with Blake, I found his "Spring" flowering on the roadway medians; I found an "Echoing Green" in every playground. Over time, many friends have found it poignant or laughable that I should have turned, in my mind, scraggly twigs into pastorals and asphalt, vest-pocket parks into greenswards. But that was the pure effect of *Songs of Innocence and Experience*. Years later, reading Traherne's "Wonder," my younger mind was explained to me.

> Harsh ragged objects were conceal'd
>   Opressions, tears, and cries,
> Sins, griefs, complaints, dissensions, weeping eyes,
>   Were hid; and only things reveal'd
> Which heavenly spirits, and the angels prize.
>   That state of innocence
> And bliss, not trades and poverties,
>   Did fill my sense
>
> ("Wonder," 25–32)

Here is the *dynamic* of innocence, creating light at the very threshold of experience, of the trades and poverties that Blake would excoriate in "London" and "The Chimney Sweeper." Energy is indeed eternal delight, and Traherne proves again and again to be the constant though concealed energy source of much of our poetry's truth. Wordsworth included. In that same spring and summer of 1969, I began to read him in one of those wonderfully inexpensive Signet editions. With Wordsworth in my pocket, I would take the train to Central Park, and soon those eight-hundred-plus acres became an unbounded Lake District to me. Years later, Traherne's "Wonder," in a single phrase, parsed and purified the pleasures I had taken (and continue to take) in "I Wandered Lonely as a Cloud" and "Ode: Intimations of Immortality." Line 46 of "Wonder" forthrightly avows: "Amazement was my bliss." Exactly—an *ars poetica* for nearly every poem I love.

It goes on. Black quickly led me to Whitman, and Wordsworth to Thoreau. Sure enough, I would, in finding Traherne, find a perfect and compact precursor of them both. In the dreadful mechanism of adolescent anonymity, I'd be uplifted by "Song of Myself," especially, and I couldn't say why, by the line "A mouse is miracle enough to stagger sextillions of infidels." I've learned to say why, thanks to Traherne. "The consideration of one soul is sufficient to convince all the atheists in the whole world" ("Centuries of Meditation: The Fourth Century," section 81).

Instead of suffering my particularity, Whitman had been urging me to be convinced, to be converted by it to an unshakeable faith. Two hundred years in advance of Whitman, there is Traherne, proposing the atomism of one soul alone, a cosmic mustard seed, an absolute sufficiency such as that which shines all throughout *Leaves of Grass*. And walking with Thoreau, seeking out the vivid forsythias in the shadows of my neighborhood's featureless row houses, I would always somehow manage to find them and, in my first god-awful poems, to celebrate them, urged on by his injunction from *A Week*: "Here or nowhere is our heaven" (Thoreau 308). Unbeknownst to Thoreau, but steadfastly both behind and ahead of him, speaks Traherne.

> Your enjoyment of the world is never right, till every
> morning you awake in Heaven . . .
> ("Centuries of Meditation: The First Century," section 28).

Blake and Wordsworth, Whitman and Thoreau expanded my place and days of origin, showing forth what, to me at least, had been heretofore hidden ecstasies, energies, and truths. They urged me to begin at the beginning—probably the most valuable lesson any poet can learn. But there was a problem, a paradox amounting to an obstacle. A poem, as I have suggested, must be a current event. The sensation of that event, its essential Easter-tide, is one of newness, of an unrestrained, illimitable immediacy. A poem moves along untrodden ways.

I quickly came to realize that, beloved though they were, these sponsors of mine were muffled and their blaze dispersed by decades and decades of critical interpretation. Shadowed by what Blake would have called "custom," by what Traherne would have called "trades," they receded into that shadow more and more as I tried to know them and to make *contact*. Equally troubling was my growing awareness of how great and how various their well-documented influence had been upon generations of poets prior to my own. It's one thing to find your models shopworn. It's quite another to feel that your inspiration itself is somehow second-hand. And that was the true and multifoliate joy of coming to Traherne. The first I heard of him was in an aside spoken by the most gloriously distracted professor with whom I ever studied. In the course of a lecture on Lawrence's *The Rainbow*, Arthur Clements referenced a passage (I have since forgotten which) of Traherne, and then moved brilliantly on. I was puzzled and delighted by the passage and made straight for the library after class. It was as if a new poet had fallen out of a tree and into my soul. Here was something entirely new to me, sweet to taste and still green with the tree. Here was immediacy writ large and an original promising to remain original. It was easy to gather as much, given the poems' constant and unabashed referencing of Adam and of Eden.

> That prospect was the gate of Heaven, that day
> The ancient light of Eden did convey
> Into my soul: I was an Adam there
>   A little Adam in a sphere . . .
>   (Traherne "Innocence," II. 49–52)

> Only what Adam did in his first estate,
>   Did I behold;
>   Hard silver and dry gold
> As yet lay underground; my blessed fate
>   Was more acquainted with the old
> And innocent delights, which he did see
> In his original simplicity.
>   (Traherne, "Eden," 29–35)

"Original simplicity" is where a poem starts when it intends to become an original. Resurrection is not a tradition; it is a sublime disruption. And a further blessing of my finding out about Traherne was the way in which he returned my first sponsors to me in their originary blaze. He disrupted the canon as I had been given to understand it. How? By being the unknown influence, the ultimate unacknowledged legislator of the art. Blake and Wordsworth, Whitman, Thoreau, and many others could never have read the poems of Traherne; but there the poems had been, radiating influence all the while. And better still, in being unknown, the secret of their influence (one wholly free of anxiety) can be kept. It remains impossible to interpret. All we can do is *feel* it. The sensation of reading once again has the luster of immediacy. When poets read, it is purity of contact they are seeking. And then new poems arise.

Poetry, like resurrection, is an intimate occasion, a new and exclusive relationship between an utterance or a soul (we may think of each as an unprecedented *breath*) and eternity. Only later does it become public information. Sovereign of all my pleasures in Traherne is the intimacy he has always offered. His poems assure me, time and again, that I am the very first to have read them. (And so, of course, are you.) Intimacy is what Traherne understands as poetry, as resurrection, as bliss. A far cry from Luther's "lonely church of one," Traherne's exclusive relationship with his God and with his reader becomes prolific. The ones and ones profuse in pleasures, becoming the oracles of themselves and of an ongoing creation whose intimacy is a new communion and, if you will, a new kind of reading.

> From one to one, in one to see all things,
> To see the King of Kings
> At once in two; to see His endless treasures
> Made all my own, myself the end
> Of all his labours! 'Tis the life of pleasures!
> To see myself His friend!
> Who of all things finds conjoin'd in him alone,
> Sees and enjoys the Holy One.
> (Traherne, "The Vision," II. 49–56)

Every poet wants to write a new poem, knowing full well that it will require a new kind of reading. Oracles are not ceased, but they must originate from within an intimacy such as Traherne's "The Vision" here describes. They have nothing to do with the interpreted or the second-hand. I am often embarrassed by the term "creative writing," and yet, because of its singular history and haphazard, because of its uniquely unequivocal and intimate affiliation with the energies of creation itself, the poetry of Thomas Traherne earns with no apparent effort every merit of that term.

> This shows a wise contrivance, and discovers
> Some great creator sitting on the throne,
> That so dispose the things for all His lovers,
> That everyone might reign like God alone.
>
> ("Ease," II. 29–32)

Every poem of Traherne's is an intimate resurrection moment. And in the reading we are raised, one by one, not unto service, as is the usual purpose of reading, but unto sovereignty. Reading, we "awake in Heaven" and find ourselves writing the poems.

Now Rest: Samuel Beckett's Creation Myth

You'll die when you hear.

—*Finnegans Wake*

Poetry delays the poem, the telling of it, outward from its center. Very much like a loving God, it is justly apprehensive at the prospect of new creation. ("Never pain to tell thy love"—William Blake.) Loving the poem before its first word, loving it literally to distraction, the best among us seem always to hesitate. And sometimes, hesitation itself becomes the art of postponement, creation resting echoic in a void just a little bit longer than possible. So it is with Homer. The story of the fall of Troy is too horrible to tell, and he does not tell it. Godly Homer pauses and amplifies at the center of the Trojan War, resting *in medias res*, where the wrath of Achilles may die, but Achilles does not. Epic simile makes for delay, and the delay is Homer's peace, his *Iliad* entire. And is it any wonder that Saint Augustine ends his *Confessions* with a loving, lengthy interpretation of the Book of Genesis, never adventuring beyond Chapter One? When last we hear of God, He is at rest, and nothing called History has begun. Keats's most perfect poem, "Ode on a Grecian Urn," begins "Thou still unravish'd bride of quietness,/Thou foster-child of silence and slow time . . .(1-2). Prosody puts full emphasis on "still." The ode goes on to amplify that stillness, in the direction of a more perfect ignorance of all events. The emptiness at the heart of the urn is echoic. And the echo takes the form of lovely creatures never to suffer throes of creation, the lapse of aftermath. Keats's poem is shown and untold. He hesitates, and everything is saved, just as any loving God would wish.

Samuel Beckett is our own time's desolate epicist of wishful thinking: desolate in that he never dissociates his very real tenderness from a ruinous eschatology; yet wishful, in that he never takes his eyes from the horizon, never ceases his vigil, no matter whether it be for a mislaid pencil stub or a featureless Messiah. Call "pencil" an old testament and "messiah" a new, and you have the exact co-ordinates of Beckett's locale—of the tree in *Waiting for Godot*, of the chair in *Endgame*, and of the spools in *Krapp's Last Tape*. In such a locale, the God writing Large and the vigilant keeping watch share an exquisite passion for delay. Having brought Creation to the brink of history, God hesitates, even luxuriates, and that is the Seventh Day. Having suffered history to the point of exhaustion, Vladimir and Estragon, Hamm and Clov and Krapp amplify the Void, preparing a place for a Sunday morning's Whomever and all his mercies. Each of them, God included, awaits the echo of himself. "Can it be Easter Week? …The final bawl lends colour to this view."(*Malone Dies*, 202) In the meantime, there is a void to prepare and to detail *ad infinitum*. Poised at the center of his great trilogy, Beckett's *Malone Dies* compasses this exacting time with epic means. There's no sense worrying the metaphors. One could say the book details the Death of God or the Death of the Author or the decease of language itself. Yes and yes and yes. What matters first and last, Alpha and Omega, are the amplified, eventually beautiful features of delay. In the delay, God preserves his splendid isolation. Messiah the revisionist and usurper is not yet. In the delay, as in the parable of the Wise and Foolish Virgins, humans fashion and unfashion trousseaus of rags and bones and shards of memory. Messiah the bridegroom and taskmaster is not yet. And in the delay, language itself lavishes time upon its syllables, puns, and portents. Messiah the silence and end of oracles is not yet. Malone is dying, but not dead. His death is inevitable. He has one last story to tell, and it too is inevitable. But his book is almost all beforehand—the life until death, the teller until the tale: that is, poetry.

If asked to summarize the plot of *Malone Dies*, the narrative ephebe could only stammer and gesticulate, troubled by non-events and numinous debris. Only in the last dozen pages or so does the gruesome story of multiple murders and escapes unfurl. And truth be told, the story is banal, a little slapstick of horrors. The life of the book is all in its heart-wrenching preamble, in Beckett's agon, whose circumference is everywhere and whose center is empty. (I cannot seem to get Saint Augustine out of my mind.) Non-events and debris are the raw materials of delay, of God's seventh day and Beckett's vigilance.

There is a choice of images. (*Malone Dies*, 190).

The prolepsis of an image is a poem, so why not choose them all! More poetry! Imagery obviates catastrophe, pushing events to the margins of time, where the inevitable is least said and soonest mended. The unravished bride remains unravished. Sprawled, like God, in a virginal cosmos, or like Malone, in his desolate leisure, perspective never withers into history. "Avid of resemblances" (197), it luxuriates in a peace that precedes and outlasts understanding. It spins out epic similes, sure enough. The poetry of *Malone Dies* shares this merit with Homer and with Chapter One of Genesis: it deconstructs deconstruction in advance, teasing postmodernism out of mind. "There is no use indicting words, they are no shoddier than what they peddle" (Beckett, 189). Exactly so. To the poet, a word is an echo not yet returned. Because of poems, the history of words remains unwritten. With Adam unfallen and Achilles very much alive, there's nothing to indict. With Malone misplacing his little pencil time and again, creation is language on a spree. "At first I did not write, I just said the thing. Then I forgot what I had said. A minimum of memory is indispensable, if one is to live really (201).With his story indefinitely postponed, Malone *lives*. Having "just said the thing," he preserves unlimited (nearly) access to what Alfred North Whitehead called "Objective immortality," that is, to the thing itself and not the memory of it, its given name. "I should really lose my pencil more often, it might do me good, I might be more cheerful, it might be more cheerful(216). Malone knows what God knew on His seventh day: the amplitude of rest, not only for himself, but for each thing unconstrained by action, unindicted by consequence. How beautiful it is that Malone considers the pencil's cheerfulness as well as his own! Much in the manner of a loving God—"I was always a great man for apples" (220)—Malone dithers in the direction of epic, which is every direction to no end. "Because in order not to die you must come and go . . ." (225).

Yet, dithering finds a way to the sublime. In a sense, what we all love most about Beckett is his mulish sublimity. In the course of non-events, there comes a moment when Malone, *in extremis*, decides to end his vigil, a vigil that by now is patently synonymous with life itself.

> One last glimpse and I feel I could slip away as happy as if I were embarking for—I nearly said Cythera, decidedly it is time for this to stop. (231)

But it does not stop. A window across the way from Malone's comes suddenly alight. Perhaps it is very late; perhaps it is very early. Nevertheless, he clearly sees two human figures "lightly clad" in pink and gold. Light and color take the form of an embrace, and Malone, all unexpectedly, has his Vision, his sublime.

> So it is not cold they are, standing so lightly clad by the open window. Ah how stupid I am, I see what it is, they must be loving each other, that must be how it is done. Good, that has done me good. (231)

Malone *in extremis* at his window and the God of Genesis looking down upon His sudden Eden share a single word: "Good." And in that word, delay finds rest and language its sublime. Everything else is amplitude. All the poetry ever since and in ages to come elaborates the time between that "Good" and its eventual, immeasurably delayed echo. Silence and emptiness are lavish with goodness. Malone has his Vision, and as always with Vision, it abolishes useless, fictive distinctions between the human and the divine. Abolition is poetry.

> To know you can do better next time, un-recognizably better, and that there is no next time, and that it is a blessing there is not, there is a thought to be going on with. (247)

"No next time" is the imperative of all creation. It is faith and helplessness, imperfection and certainty combined. It "is a thought to be going on with," if only because it keeps the unravished bride *and* her pursuing bridegroom (i.e., Edenic Adam and Eve, the lightly clad couple in the window, the poet and the poem) one full step ahead of aftermath for good. Malone confides all this to his little book for as long as an empty page remains.

> This exercise-book is my life, this big child's exercise book, it has taken me a long time to resign myself to that. And yet I shall not throw it away. For I want to put down in it, for the last time, those I have called to my help, but ill, so that they did not understand, so that they may cease with me. Now rest. (267)

We are big children with an empty page or more to fill. A myth to be going on with.

Poésie Pure and Others

> *A virginity which, in its solitude, faced with the transparency of a commensurate gaze, has itself been as it were fragmented into its component whitenesses, one upon the next, the wedding—proofs of the Idea.*

> —Stéphane Mallarmé, "Mystery in Literature"

Poetry is a solitude not alone in its unrefined purity. More than any of the modern poets' acknowledged masters, Mallarmé espoused (his words were *ever* wedding proofs) and sought to embody a pure poetry, a spontaneous decorum and atmosphere of language entirely sufficient to the white life of Idea. The order of words would transpire beyond syntax, in a transparency so perfect as to abolish the distinctions between perceiver and perceived, between writing and reading. (Transparency is invisible but not obscure, mysterious but freely available.) He imagined a pure gaze, one innocent of any violation or advantage. The solitude of poetry would be a new world, a further Eden, and every poem would constitute unto itself a superlative state. When I think of such things, when I happen upon such vocabulary, I cannot help but imagine an America, and sure enough, America's own pure poets rush into my mind. As befits our polity, the superlative states of American poetry are wildly various; we practice many purities. There have been innumerable unrefined solitudes since the one at Walden Pond. Nevertheless, Mallarmé remains our practical friend and a model to our practice. To proliferate the virgin whitenesses, the wildnesses, to disperse perfections without destroying them (fragments remain intact and phenomenal when wedded to a gaze) to preserve transparency in all candor and intimacy—these are ideals familiar to American poetry. The pure poets of America are crazy for mystery as it comes freely to mind and to hand in the clear sunshine.

I choose three: Hart Crane, Joseph Ceravolo, and Barbara Guest. My principle of selection is pleasure, pure and simple, but not exclusively my own. Distinct as they are, each of these poets is deeply *pleasured* in his or her own words, and in this essay I hope to emphasize the pleasures as well as the rigors of purity. I do not like to think of poetry as consolation. Pain is real, but the pure poem outspeeds pain, or, perhaps, outsmarts it. Velocity is a kind of wisdom and an analgesic too. I was first drawn to Barbara Guest because of her courage in using the phrase "Stupid Physical Pain" as the title for a perfectly ebullient poem. And I was first drawn to Crane by the image of his spinning a recording of Ravel's "Bolero" over and over again. To speak of Crane is to speak of inward velocities; he is the holy dervish of our jazz and slang. As for Ceravolo, anyone whose masterpiece is titled "Ho Ho Ho Caribou" has clearly broken through the impurities of argument and metaphor into a place where the wild things are delighted to be wild. These three, among our poets, most amply and most vividly detail the place or purity in praxis Mallarmé could love. In his essay "Literature," Paul Valéry, the most tender arbiter of the great *Symboliste*, foresaw them all though, unbeknownst to him, upon a farther shore:

> Their poetry bears the mark of this practice. It is a translation, a *faithless beauty*—faithless to what is not in accord with the exigencies of a pure language. (151).

Breaking faith, so boldly, so tenderly, with argument and with metaphor, Hart Crane, Joseph Ceravolo, and Barbara Guest practice the translation of beauty into beauty in pleasures that are True.

It is a pure sound that resounds in the midst of noise. It is a perfectly executed fragment of an edifice. (Paul Valéry, "The Memories of a Poem" 160).

To Hart Crane, purity came as a release from epic, as a blessed break from the ambitions of "For the Marriage of Faustus and Helen" and from the elusive architectonics of *The Bridge*. He was a poet who broke his heart, but not his gift, upon high modernism. Thus it is that I find myself most happily drawn to his last poems: those collected in *Key West* and, thanks to Marc Simon's brilliant editorial work, the later fragments now available to all. Schooled, like most, in Hart Crane's anthology pieces, I love to remember the sweet perplexity and then the buoyancy I felt when first I read "The Mango Tree."

The Mango Tree

Let them return, saying you blush again for the great
Great-grandmother. It's all like Christmas.

When you sprouted Paradise a discard of chewing-gum took place. Up jug to musical, hanging jug just gay spiders yoked you first,—silking of shadows good underdrawers for owls.

First-plucked before and since the Flood, old hypnotisms wrench the golden boughs. Leaves spatter dawn from emerald cloud-sprockets. Fat final prophets with lean bandits crouch: and dusk is close

under your noon,
you Sun-heap, whose
ripe apple-lanterns gush history, recondite lightnings, irised.
O mister Señor
missus Miss
Mademoiselle
with baskets
Maggy, come on

Here is the purity of child's play in its full maturity. Risibly Rimbaldian in its references to Christmas and the Flood and, via those golden boughs, glad to blow a raspberry at its abandoned high modernism, "The Mango Tree" is nevertheless instantly far beyond or far above satire in its immediate permissions: "Let them return"; there's a further paradise in a wad of gum. And there the wonderful hyphens (as in "cloud-sprockets" and "apple lanterns") spell a new technology of the sacred, as simple, as portable, as freely inclusive as "baskets." A pure poem is unremitting in its inclusiveness, having excluded from itself the arguments that tether its figures to figures of speech. So quickly, "The Mango Tree" accomplishes a sun-drenched purity equal to the most beautiful passages in Gertrude Stein's *Tender Buttons* yet free of that great book's programmatic emphases. "Maggy, come on" is a summons to new circumstance where the poem says, and needs to say, no more.

Under the rigor of purity, dissipation becomes one of the virtues of new circumstance. Valéry's "perfectly executed fragment of an edifice" suggests a different integrity, a wholeness broken free from entirety and gaily underway. Where a poem needs to say no more, it is at liberty to say as much and whatever it likes. Purity turns out to be an antinomian practice, and in what to me is Hart Crane's most perfect fragment, "Tenderness and Resolution," the rebellion of words themselves against the bondage of rhetoric and definition succeeds almost before it begins, so effortlessly does the poem unburden itself of argument.

> Tenderness and resolution
> What is our life without a sudden pillow—
> What is death without a ditch?
>
> The harvest laugh of bright Apollo
> And the flint tooth of Sagittarius
> Rhyme from the same jaw—(closing cinch by cinch)
> And pocket us who, somehow, do not follow,
> As though we knew those who are variants—
> Charms—that each by each refuse the clinch
>
> With desperate propriety, whose name is writ
> In wider letters than the alphabet, —
> Who is now left to vary the Sanscrit
> Pillowed by

My wrist in the vestibule of time—who
Will hold it—wear the keepsake, dear, of time—
Return the mirage on a coin that spells
Something of sand and sun the Nile defends . . . (1-17)

Crane's opening stanza embodies an instance of conjunctions
so pure as to be inarguable and so comprehensive as to thrive
beyond the question of their questions. What virtues do not fall
somewhere between tenderness and resolution?

What experience does not transpire somewhere between life and death? And from thence, conjunctions dissipate
widely into the permissions of themselves: a god and a constellation; desperation and propriety; a careless rhyming (cinch
and clinch, writ and Sanscrit) nevertheless perfected by new
circumstance, the "wider letters than the alphabet." Purity is
thus shown to be a purposeful though effortless dissipation and
expense, "pillowed by" the poet's plain refusal to follow a line
of argument where charms will work quite well. Crane's is the
supra-logic of a river . . . say, the Nile. A river intends to reach
the sea, though its intentions are unknowable. If purity is, after all, a "mirage," it is well defended by the spell of words set
free by a poet into their magical "variants."

> *Poetry is only literature reduced to the essence of its*
> *active principle.*
>
> —Paul Valéry, "Literature" 148

The active principle in the poetry of Joseph Ceravolo
is a quiet purgation of the condescending and distancing Picturesque from poetry's worshipful encounters with Nature. Of
Ceravolo's poems, mentor and friend Kenneth Koch has written that they "make no gestures or appeals outside themselves."
This is quite literally true, primarily because Ceravolo never
regards Nature as an *outside*, and thus his relations with it are
never merely social. Rhetoric is a social network of unnatu-
ral courtesies. Landscape is the rhetoric of the Picturesque, a
backward arrangement of energies whose only motion can be
forward. Ceravolo's poems are purely sited, not in landscape,
but in pure Space from which the human and human relation-

ships have not been banished but *into* which, rather, they have been released. Unbounded, Ceravolo's vision/version of purity discovers new species and a new nature spun effortlessly out of energies of escape. (In another era, in another context, I might call such purity apocalyptic, for in his own gentle way, Ceravolo shares much with St. John of Patmos.) In Ceravolo's most noted and anthologized poem, "Ho Ho Ho Caribou," hermetic spaces of intimacy are wilded by vastation, all the while preserving their intimacy. Suddenly, the caribou is a domestic animal, even as domestic life reveals the wilderness of its perfection. Here are the first two sections:

1
Leaped at the caribou.
My son looked at the caribou.
The kangaroo leaped on the
fruit tree. I am a white
man and my children
are hungry
which is like paradise.
The doll is sleeping.
It lay down to creep into
the plate.
It was clean and flying.

2
Where you . . . the axes
are. Why is this home so
hard. So much
like the sent over the
courses below the home
having a porch.
Felt it on my gate in the place
where caribous jumped
over. Where geese sons
and pouches of daughters look at
me and say "I'm hungry
daddy." (1-23)

The initial and initiating leap (of faith, as with Kierkegaard? into cleanness, as with Rupert Brooke?) is a soft peril immediately forgotten in the pure speech of newness. Kangaroos move through trees. Whiteness and hunger constitute a kind of paradise. Children become new species of children: waterfowl sons and marsupial daughters. This peaceable kingdom, though unprecedented, is instantly prolific. Intimacy proves expansive when its every nature is new, and along the way, Ceravolo proves a new destiny—not manifest, but manifested—for purity in a poem. "Ho Ho ho Caribou" gives evidence of the pure poem's immeasurable spiritual *capacity* where purity is the measure of every word's uncontrollable rebirth. The poem ends

10
Like a flower, little light, you open
and we make believe
we die. We die all around
you like a snake in a
well and we come up out
of the warm well and
are born again out of dry
mammas, nourishing mammas, always
holding you as I
love you and am
revived inside you, but
die in you and am
never born again in
the same place; never
stop! (112-26)

This is neither a jeweled purity nor an astral one. This is infinite, but very near. Rebirth sets out from Pure Land to the next Pure Land, unresting but not restless. I can find no other word to describe the spiritual substance and event of this stanza but *renovation*. Ceravolo's new Nature remains new by the constant renovation of its most intimate relations, each of which is nurtured in, and as, a poem.

The brilliance of these crystalline constructions, so pure, and so perfectly finished in every part, fascinated me. They have not the transparency of glass, no doubt; but in that they somehow break habits of mind on their facets and on their concentrated structure, what is called their obscurity is only, in reality, their refraction.

—Paul Valéry, "On Mallarmé" 215

In the splendidly diverse company of America's pure poets, none so entirely and self-effacingly accomplishes a perfected fascination as does Barbara Guest. She is the Mallarmé of us—and more. All her finest poems (and they are many) present structures of concentration without pressure, of density without darkness or unwieldy mass. Having read them, one feels a buoyancy requiring neither ocean nor air; it is as if the vastness of the whiteness of the page had itself proved elemental. Guest goes the pre-Socratics one better: earth, air, water, fire, page. In "Red Lilies," from *Moscow Mansions*, surely one of the least celebrated of America's great books, every line cleaves the whiteness without violence and then flowers there. As you come to the line breaks, think of William Carlos Williams's masterful noticing in *Spring and All*: "each petal ends in / an edge" ("The rose is obsolete," 2-3).

> Someone has remembered to dry the dishes;
> they have taken the accident out of the stove.
> Afterward lilies for supper; there
> the lines in front of the window
> are rubbed on the table of stone
>
> The paper flies up
> then down as the wind
> repeats, repeats its birdsong.
>
> Those arms under the pillow
> the burrowing arms they cleave
> at night as the tug kneads water
> calling themselves branches
> (Barbara Guest, "Red Lilies" 1-12)

Each of these lines does indeed show a facet to the eye, a smooth and independent plane. Yet, each is also a contiguity—a continuity with no insistence beyond its present fact and bright locale. The contiguity is transformational: a "someone" becomes "they," even as "the accident" somehow begets "lilies" and as flying paper learns to sing. Transformations do break habits of mind, but they do it inarguably in the purity of their instant aftermaths.

> The tree is you
> the blanket is what warms it
> snow erupts from thistle;
> the snow pours out of you.
>
> A cold hand on the dishes
> placing a saucer inside
> he who undressed for supper
> gliding that hair to the snow
>
> The pilot light
> went out on the stove
>
> The paper folded like a napkin
> other wings flew into the stone.
> ("Red Lilies" 13-24)

"The tree is you," which is to say a new species, as does Ceravolo, only now perfectly isolate in its singular and crystalline domestic plane. Thus is Guest an integral Ovid whose metamorphoses take no time at all and are already in place, safe at home for supper.

The pure poem is beyond all rumors of itself. In *Miniatures*, one of the very last collections Guest published in her lifetime, we find a poem titled "Noisetone." The word is neither neologism nor splice; rather, as a reading of the poem shows, it is a natural consequence of purity underway. In an atmosphere of absolute qualities—qualities arising *from* but never confined *to* particulars—pure attentions are taken up into the new which is their nature. Thus can a noise accomplish tonality while retaining all the newness of its noise. And the noise is a color too.

Noisetone

    Each artist embarks on a personal search.
       An artist may take introspective refreshment from green.

Or so they say in Barcelona when air is dry.
    In our country it is a water sprinkler that hints, "rinsed green."
       Colors often break themselves into separate hues

of noisetone.   In a Barcelona cabaret where green is overtaken,
it is stirred into the mint color of drink.
    The spirit is lifted among primary colors. Nine rows of color.

    The future writ in white spaces.

"Each artist," "An artist," "Or so they say"—singularity dissipates in the rumor poetry outspeeds. Greenness escapes from green, becoming sound too. This is not mere synesthesia. This is a wholly new stave and palette. And here, spirit regains its proper medium, that is, the "primary." Barbara Guest announces, in spare declaration, the prophetic power of purity that arises from, and through, a continuous prime. In such a medium, poems are not objects anymore. They are individual trajectories and individual destinies: colors bound for the white space where futurity is inscribed. Purity turns out to be, in its uncontrollable, careless diversity, perfectly suited to an American ideal. The pure poets of America speak the spirit of matter, a superlative nation.

Barbara Guest: A Family of Mountaineers / on "Roses"

A Family of Mountaineers

He was particularly indignant against the almost universal use of the word idea in the sense of notion or opinion, when it is clear that idea can only signify something of which an image can be formed in the mind.

—James Boswell, The Life of Samuel Johnson

Exceptionalism is a circumstance purely—one of quiet attention to one truth just as that truth begins to change. The Tea Party might be amazed, but American poetry has always taken exceptionalism to be the natural consequence of its piety before the wilding of the New. Our poems are wholly given to laud the exceptional minutes of real change. "Terrific units are on an old man" (15) John Ashbery avers in "Two Scenes," the opening poem of his debut collection, and he concludes "In the evening / Everything has a schedule, if you can find out what it is" (17-18). An *opening* poem surely, "Two Scenes" redoubles the instants of its gaze as objects seen remake the scenic grammars of juxtaposition into some things, rich and strange. "News" rhymes perfectly with "noise;" and as "the day was warm and pleasant" (7), it becomes proper and irresistible to say "we see you in your hair, / Air resting around the tips of mountains" (8-9). This is not obscurity. This is exceptionalism purely taking note. Exceptionalism is where we start from.

The precedent is as old as the Book of Genesis, which begins with an exception to the Rule.

Barbara Guest, like Ashbery a poet of the New York School's first and most vivid generation, begins her own debut with a title poem, "The Location of Things." Twinning "Two Scenes," it fronts emphatic change with eyes and not with grammars. "Why from this window am I watching leaves?" Wherever the eye alights, the accent falls, freely. Every word might be the exceptionalist. For example: "why from *this* window" puts the case of one out of many, or perhaps one most (or least) of all. Transparency trumps structure. For example: "why . . . am *I* watching leaves?" queries a possible distraction, or visitation. From there it is hardly any distance at all to Vision and the visionary mode. I'm going too far, I know, but I've been invited. The very words with which the poem declares its location *dis*locate—one by one and by one—the emphases. And the soul of exceptionalism is the absolute freedom to emphasize at will. It uses a grammar beyond grammars. (Here I am reminded of a beautiful phrase from Ann Lauterbach's "Boy Sleeping;"—"I am coming with you nevertheless and because" (24). I take those words to be self-evident.) Beyond grammars, words go free. They make a dash, as Dickinson's so often did. The last word on the line is "leaves." The noun, plural, inclines towards a verb, and there it goes. We are left with a question. Location has opted for furthering and for elsewhere. Wherever the eye alights, it goes free.

When objects seen are not for one moment delayed by the scenic, that is, the captivating mind, wonderful geographies become the order of the day.

> . . . am I to find a lake under the table
> or a mountain beside my chair
> and will I know the minute water produces lilies
> or a family of mountaineers scales the peak?
> (Guest, "The Location of Things" 7-10)

This is an America America never meant to say. This is a wilderness country discovered wholly in the minutes of one uncanny emphasis: the poem. Each word, as if to reference Ashbery's stanza, is a "terrific unit," numbering the impossible union of inward and outward, nevertheless and because of a poetic line whose syntactic interior is suddenly engrossed by mountaineers. The exceptional happens. At times, it appears miraculous. At times, it occurs as a matter of fact, in a portrait of a boy having his breakfast outdoors with mountains visible in the distance beside his chair, painted by Fairfield Porter. To the exceptionalist, miracles are matters of fact, and certain facts, such as the painting by Porter, simply miraculous. The self-evident has something more than a metaphor in store.

> . . . It reminds me
> of pictures in restaurants, the exchange of hunger
> for thirst, art for decoration and in a hospital
> love for pain suffered beside the glistening rhododen-
>   dron
> under the crucifix.
>
> (Guest, "The Location of Things" 14-18)

Beyond or, rather, *apart* from metaphor, are vivid exchanges to which the attention of the exceptionalist bears terrific witness. Then arrives something further than witness: a wilding. Alerted to exchange, the poem crosses over, quietly, into a new territory. (Quietism is what distinguishes the New York School from every other American avant-garde: the *panache* of piety.) Love is on offer for pain. A flower glistens at the foot of the cross. Not figurative, but literal, these are states of being, emblems of self-evidence in the new nature, their natural habitat. Alert to exchange as to a new species of empowerment, the poem emphasizes and is emphasized in its turn by remarkable *locations* of change.

> . . . The street, the street bears light
> and shade on its shoulders, walks without crying,
> turns itself into another and continues, even
> cantilevers this barroom atmosphere into a forest
> and sheds its leaves on my table
> carelessly . . .
>
> (Guest, "The Location of Things" 18-23)

Here is power to which metaphor can only allude. Here, care-lessness is the prerogative of the Exceptional. Guest shows it also to be the instance of tenderness and relief.

"The Location of Things" goes on to become in itself bright evidence of exactly how the exceptional pluralizes all en-tities, dispatching numberless singularities each upon its unique errand to the wilderness. (It is only surprising for a little while, and then wonderful, to realize that the New York School, more than any American avant-garde, takes up the Puritan task.) Guest depicts an ecstasy of pronouns against a pure background of transparent window glass.

> That head against the window
> how many times one has seen it. Afternoons
> of smoke and wet nostrils,
> the perilous makeup on her face and on his,
> numerous corteges. The water's lace creates funerals
> it makes us see someone we love in an acre of grass. (27-32)

The aftermath of ecstasy is, for once, not familiar sorrow but extravagant nature newly born(e) by love out of death. "If you want me again look for me under your boot-soles."

It is the way of miracles to be miraculous, that is, to em-body exceptions to those very rules which make them exception-al. This is the American mystery. This is the way in which ex-ceptionalism proves the one and only Democratic Vista on offer just now. Guest ends her poem with a final extravagance, an op-eratic gesture which would have thrilled our Whitman through and through.

> . . . I hand you
> from my prompter's arm this shako,
> wandering as I am into clouds and air
> rushing into darkness as corridors
> who do not fear the melancholy of the stair. (36-40)

Her errand is new. The changes underway are not fearsome, and the climb effortless. It is hardly any distance to Mount Vision after all.

Roses

"painting has no air . . ."

—Gertrude Stein

That there should never be air
in a picture surprises me.
It would seem to be only a picture
of a certain kind, a portrait in paper
or glued, somewhere a stickiness
as opposed to a stick-to-it-ness
of another genre. It might be
quite new to do without
that air, or to find oxygen
on the landscape line
like a boat which is an object
or a shoe which never floats
and is stationary.
                              Still there
are certain illnesses that require
air, lots of it. And there are nervous
people who cannot manufacture
enough air and must seek
for it when they don't have plants,
in pictures. There is the mysterious
traveling that one does outside
the cube and this takes place
in air.
                              It is why one develops
an attitude toward roses picked
in the morning air, even roses
without sun shining on them.
The roses of Juan Gris from which
we learn the selflessness of roses
existing perpetually without air,
the lid being down, so to speak,
withal a 1912 fragrance sifting
to a left corner where we read
"La Merveille" and escape.

The only time I ever planned to spend an extended time abroad, I sent a little box of books ahead of me: books chosen to be my America, should I have need of America. The box was lost. So, for many months, the only homemade poems to hand were two that I had typed and folded into my wallet for the airplane ride: Robert Creeley's "Flowers," from *Pieces*, and Barbara Guest's "Roses," from *Moscow Mansions*. I had not planned them as a bouquet but, rather, as an atmosphere, a fragrance of transport. About the Creeley poem, I have already written a little essay, "Proper Rites," and it appears in *Invisible Green*. Of "Roses," I want to write here my continuing pleasure in the atmosphere Guest makes, there.

The poem opens with an epigram from Gertrude Stein—"*painting has no air*"—immediately, albeit tenderly, refused. Guest begins, "That there should never be air / in a picture surprises me. The quiet revolution, that is, the literal turning-round of this statement, is indispensably American. Announcing the sudden freedom of surprise (where someone such as Breton, perhaps, might have spoken of "convulsion") "Roses" breathes new air—air that, only a moment before, simply wasn't there. A little gasp of surprise liberates both poet and reader from prior circumstance. And then a few lines farther on, Guest furthers new liberty as new logic:

> It might be
> quite new to do without
> that air, or to find oxygen
> on the landscape line
> like a boat which is an object
> or a shoe which never floats
> and is stationary.

The discovery of oxygen in so radically simple a simile as "like a boat which is an object / or a shoe which never floats" declares new reason and has, already and effortlessly, escaped the confines of old logic. This is one of Barbara Guest's most singular and sustained contributions to the American avant-garde: a quietist's vastation and a whispered over-throw. As in Fairfield Porter's gestural realism, "Roses" finds its figures hovering in free space among other figures equally free. The boat and shoe are here together, each on a line of its own. One is a flower, and the other is one flower more. The poem breathes them in. And out. And as with breathing, effortlessness is also the abiding mystery of life.

> There is the mysterious
> traveling that one does outside
> the cube and this takes place
> in air.

Air is an exit strategy and a transport, too. It is an exterior freely available. We take it in, and its fragrance frees us.

> It is why one develops
> an attitude toward roses picked
> in the morning air, even roses
> without sun shining on them.
> The roses of Juan Gris from which
> we learn the selflessness of roses
> existing perpetually without air,
> the lid being down, so to speak,
> withal a 1912 fragrance sifting
> to the left corner where we read
> "La Merveille" and escape.

Here, as before, and more widely, "Roses" makes a revolution without violence, avowing a partisanship only for the liberty of all things. The marvel of existence without air *is* air as surely as, almost exactly one century prior to *Moscow Mansions*, the old sun proved to be a morning star. Reading and writing and roses escape together with their singular eternities intact. Stein is refuted and furthered. The morning air of 1912 aspires to new roses, today. Such a marvel, so softly spoken, is Barbara Guest's American Beauty, dearly needful now.

Ballads of the Provisional City:
James Schuyler's *A Few Days* and
John Ashbery's *Selected Poems*

Variety has always enjoyed the status of sacrament in New York poems. It was Frank O'Hara, the school's incandescent icon and iconographer, the poet whose poems made an aesthetic of energy and of compassionate involvement in the life and lives of art as they become confluent in one life (the poem's), who conferred that status. His tombstone reads "Grace to be born and live as variously as possible." The life in his work found that grace often enough to make a good number of his poems indispensable signifiers of our time. *A Few Days* finds more than a considerable, moving measure of that same grace. And *Selected Poems* offers nothing less than a constellation of variety, a constant discovery of grace abounding.

It is a sad fact that variousness and grace are easily misconstrued. The work of the New York Poets has often been dismissed as lacking in proper seriousness, in consistent, accessible form, because their poems shift discourse and attitude with neither warning nor apology. They clothe the private objects of private worlds in the mantle of archetype. They afford the colloquialisms and codes of private language the authority of high speech. And they do not hesitate to display the trivial beside the archetypal, nor do they shrink from combining private and public speech in framing utterances as near to the inconsistent heart of living language as they can manage. The art that illuminates Schuyler's and Ashbery's poems (and which illuminates *A Nest of Ninnies*, the elegantly various comic novel they authored together) is the art of inclusion, one that seeks to devise what Ashbery called in "As One Put Drunk into the Packet-Boat" a "ballade / That takes in the whole world" (25-26). The timid aesthetic of the New Critics endorsed a morbid exclusion. Propounders of that exclusion continue to find it easy to dismiss the subtle counterpoint of New York poetry as mere facility, mere urbane improvisation, just as similar critics in the realm of the visual arts found it easy to dismiss the canvases of the Abstract Expressionists and Gestural Painters (the artists most often and most accurately associated with the New York Poets) as works children might successfully replicate. The rigorous simplicity of Porter's portraits is not improvised, and no accidental facility can account for the range of feeling they express. The now frantic, now placid reaches of a Pollock canvas are not just maps of contingency. They are an expansive field of one man's endeavor to accommodate his entire sensibility and experience. So it is that Schuyler's plainly conversational, matter-of-fact poems are actually meticulously, heart-breakingly faithful life studies of the numinous ephemera of daily life. So it is that Ashbery's diverse, hauntingly dissonant voices join in recitals of grand ballades, songs aspiring to the grand asymmetries of the worlds they praise.

I have said that what joins the poetry of Schuyler and Ashbery is a variousness (at the level of pure language as well as at that of theme and intention) arising from a working principle of inclusion. They are cosmopolitan poets, surely, worldly in that they bar nothing from their writing on any preconceived grounds, in that they are willing, as O'Hara was, to find a single moment animated and made legible as much by Sixth Avenue laborers as by *Poems* by Pierre Reverdy. Yet, the phrase "New York Poem" is not simply the name for a limitless verbal container. All things, even words themselves, change upon entering the unique structure of any one poem. And an openness to all perception and experience does not imply that all perceptions and experiences are ultimately equivalent. Schuyler's openness engenders one body of work. Ashbery's another. Both practice inclusion, yet the sea changes that befall things upon their entrance into Schuyler's poems are clearly distinguishable from those which befall the chosen or discovered objects of Ashbery's ballades. A school of poetry is a provisionally useful idea or category, but good poets and good poems remain ideas of their own, categories unto themselves. The beautiful title poem of *A Few Days* recognizes the distinctions between the sensibilities of the two poets, the two friends, and better than any scholar has yet done, defines those distinctions as they characterize the products of those sensibilities.

Of himself, Schuyler writes, ". . , I have always been / more interested in truth than in imagination . . ." (*A Few Days* 73). Indeed, it is truth—the quotidian, phenomenal truth of things as they look on windowsills, of friends and lovers as they appear in certain real rooms, of the flowers in particular fields—that fills Schuyler's poetry and to which he devotes his fixed, careful attention. Schuyler loves to name names—of flowers, of buildings, of friends—and much of his work's power originates in the totemic power of names as they are disclosed in their unabashed contexts. Of Ashbery, friend and confrere, Schuyler writes, ". . . John is devoted to the impossible" (*A Few Days* 78). And indeed, Ashbery is our laureate of the impossible, a magical realist of a poet whose attention is devoted to the fantastic events that ensue once the imagination truly seizes the world. He *invents* names and occasions to bear them, though he invents not out of the world, but into it, as Stevens did.

At a quick glance, Ashbery's would seem to be the more glamourous, more ambitious enterprise. Not surprisingly, it has received the lion's share of the critical attention given to the New York School. Compared to Ashbery's, Schuyler's poetry can seem all too easy, a passive catalogue, a prosaic daybook. Schuyler himself was aware of this, and in one interview (*The American Poetry Review* Vol. 14, No. 2) offered an anecdote as commentary upon such hasty, unflattering comparisons:

> Once, I was walking through the slush in Washington Square with Frank [O'Hara] going to a bar, and we were talking about our own poetry, when suddenly, Frank said, in his very bitter tone, "Let's face it, John's the

poet!" which rather pissed me off, because I thought I
was a poet too. (7–8)

I am happy to agree. Schuyler *is* a poet too, as valuable in his
way as his more celebrated colleague. His faithful attention has
resulted in poems as memorable, as dedicated to the mortal
world as those conjured by Ashbery's magical sorties into the
real. I am happy to have both poets. No one can reassure me of
the dignity of ordinary life in real places as Schuyler can. And
no one can convince me of the fantastic possibilities that halo
places and lives as Ashbery can. Who would want less of either
dignity or possibility? Who would not rejoice at the published
increase of either?

An essay about a single collection of poems by one poet
and about the selected life's work of another may seem hopeless to balance and likely to perpetuate the false notion of James
Schuyler as the second fiddle of the New York School. Still, the
apparent imbalance is, in a curiously good way, in keeping with
the distinctions I see between these two major poets. Schuyler's persona is one that rejoices in transience, in the differ-
ences between one hour and the next. It is a persona that likes
to engage life by moments as they arrive and that does not care
to urge its loving attention to one into any final vision of them
all. For Schuyler, every day is its own big picture—in the anticipation, the living, and the remembrance of it. Any intimation
of a grand design is as subject to transience as the moment in
which it is intimated. Hence, the absolute rightness of the title
A Few Days. Rightly attended to and lived by Schuyler, a few days
figure many certain worlds and a full volume.

The themes that link these certain worlds are constants
of Schuyler's work and fundamental to the New York aesthetic. The complementary roles played by nature and art in the
shaping of the poet's self and utterance are continuously as-
serted and portrayed. New York Poetry is cosmopolitan, not
urban, and defines a good part of itself in a focus shifting between aspects of the natural world and the jigsaw closet dra-
mas of city life and the cultural round. (It is well to remember
that both Schuyler and Ashbery came of age in the "holy land"

of Western New York State.) Neither poet was New York City bred, and both are as familiar with and as responsive to wild-flowers as to Monet's water lilies. And behind this shifting focus is another constant—the urgency of mortality. *A Few Days* is a book of courageous poems, characterized by a domestic sort of courage. It bravely champions the validity and excellence of private life and private feelings in the face of an increasingly insistent mortality that threatens to overwhelm and, in overwhelming, to negate both. Death forms the continuous background of *A Few Days*, but against that darkness, the illuminated figures of individual poems blaze as fleeting but memorable pyrotechnics.

The poems explicitly conceived in nature celebrate the poet's faithful consciousness of nature's beauty and its transience. His fidelity allows him a share of the beauty. His mortality guarantees his share of transience.

> The window is filled
> with leaves! So different
> from my urban view
> in stony-hearted New York.
> I love leaves, so green,
> so still, then
> all ashimmer. Would
> I like to live here? I
> don't know: it's
> far from friends
> (for me) and others
> I depend on. But
> It's awfully nice to visit,
> a whaling port
> like Sag Harbor, Long Island.
> ("The Rose of Marion"11-25)

> Each truss of seemingly
> myriad, four-petalled
> flowers of that color
> (lilac) Persia dreamed up . . .
> . . . I love them as

they are, seeming so
permanent, yet even
more transient than we!
Now I think I'll have
a sniff of lilac,
then eat a wedge
of rhubarb pie:
rhubarb and lilacs:
could life hold more?
Perhaps:
there is, for instance,
Helena.

> ("Lilacs" 13-29)

The mortal speaker is ever a visitor, his tone always provisional. It is the power of affection that admits him into such plain,
candid sympathy with leaves and flowers, just as it is the power
of affection that draws him back to the more complicated, human beauty of city rooms and friends.

And there are poems that explore the origins of affection. The awareness of his own and everything's transience in-
tensifies the motive to love and love's wonder. It makes the dear
friend dearer still.

I can easily believe that I
am fifty-eight, but that you
are forty fills me with wonder! I remember
how young you seemed (and were)
the first time I met you . . .
. . . and though I don't
see you often I think about
you a lot:
for your birthday I would like
to send you a bunch of lilies
of the valley, which mean,
in the language of flowers,
"I love you since long."

> ("Dear Joe" 1-6, 26-33)

This awareness makes a beloved place's very name a joy and victory to speak.

> And now the sun shines
> down in silent brightness,
> on me and my possessions,
> which I have named,
> New York.
>> ("Moon" 24-28)

Mortality drives Schuyler to name his sacred names, to seek to tell his loves, and the very telling constitutes the poems' brave, inspiring flourish.

This flourish, in the very best poems from *A Few Days*, lends grandeur to mortality and to the constant passing of worlds. In them, affection sees into the heart of mortal change and finds that heart full. While its affections turn, the heart lives, and the turning describes an eternal return, a cycle of constancy in which no dear thing is ever finally lost or abandoned. In "Autumn Leaves," the poet, regarding the immitigable changes of seasons, finds himself suddenly and instructively reunited with his lost friend Frank O'Hara.

> Then we come to a fence
> where one who has given
> his life to poetry leans.
> Next to him a sign proclaims
> ETERNAL HAPPINESS. Am I
> dreaming about Frank again?
> Frank among the leaves
> all turning, turning, turning. (15-22)

It is an old theme, perhaps our culture's grandest. Mortality's cyclical form is a form of immortality, a heart's eternally returning wheel. Riding that wheel is O'Hara, the luminous advocate of change, proclaiming eternal happiness with it all. "Autumn Leaves" is a miniature elegy, one of the finest pieces Schuyler ever wrote.

Change bears affection into the future as well. There, the poet's flourish is a thanksgiving for new loves revealed. In "Autumn Leaves" the consciousness of change directs the poet's imagination back towards one lost. In "O Sleepless Night" the imagination moves towards one newly found. The poem opens on a sense memory of Schuyler's former happiness in living with the painter Fairfield Porter and his family. Porter's ghost haunts all of *A Few Days*. The charmed, literal quality of his painterly vision matched Schuyler's poetic one beautifully, and Schuyler often grieves over the homes lost to him—in Maine, on Long Island, in the circle of the painter's kindred mind—since Porter's death. Yet, as in "Autumn Leaves," sadness yields to wonder, and the sleepless night minutely chronicled in this poem ends in the morning of desire, of the embarkation upon new love and new love's restless anticipation.

> I mean to say, why
> Oh, tell me why
> why do you not lie beside me
> entwined in one another's arms
> my head upon your pliant marble shoulder
> you asleep and me awake,
> decked beside me
> body pressed body to body?
> Tom . . .
> ("O Sleepless Night" 201-209)

Change is the guarantor of the past and future. Trusting his inspiration to it, Schuyler maintains himself as a vulnerable poet of glad, astonished possibilities.

The closing, title poem of this book gathers a host of possibilities together, just as did the title poem of Schuyler's Pulitzer Prize winning *The Morning of the Poem*. And like "The Morning of the Poem," it takes as its form the content of a discrete passage of days, the minutiae of which become the characters of a provisional legend. The plot of the poem is itself the stuff of legend. The poet travels to his childhood home and is, as Schuyler so often was, a visitor in his own life. He details the sad decline of his aged mother and the estrangement he feels inside the routines of his brother's family. These details exert the pressure of mortality upon him, and he returns to New York City, closing a circle. Like any number of legendary travelers, he returns to origin only to find it changed, to find that it holds no place for him, and that he must travel back into the life improvised since his original departure.

Once back in the city, Schuyler re-entered the round of his days, a circle lately made smaller by illness and age, but still enriched by a feeling for friends (including Ashbery) and for the various life of art. It would be silly to isolate any single passage from the body of "A Few Days." The poem gathers force through a quiet process of accretion, and no passage can be adequately felt outside of this process. Suffice it to say that it is all vintage Schuyler, made even more compelling by its struggle against the necessary diminishment of life and by its undiminished urge to love and wonder.

The poem and the book end upon Schuyler's receiving word of his mother's death. I can't help but contradict myself a little and quote the last lines. Even out of context, they shine with Schuyler's particular light:

And so I won't be
there to see my Maney
unearthed beside
my stepfather:
once when I was
home a while ago
I said I realized
that in his way he
loved me. "He did
not," my mother said.
"Burton hated you."
The old truth-teller!
She was so proud
in her last dim
years (ninety years
are still
a few days) to be

longest-lived of
the Slaters: for-
getting her mother
was the Slater, she
a Connor:
Margaret Daisy Connor Schuyler Ridenour,
rest well,
the weary journey done. (535-59)

Rejecting easy consolations and the convention formulae of comfort, asserting that even "ninety years / are still / a few days," Schuyler ends with a benediction. He names his mother's names and so sees her off into eternity. With the same gesture, he sees *A Few Days* off into the body of his accomplished work. It lives there, a name to be named by any that value what poetry values.

A critic's assertion of value is a matter both more and less pressing as he comes to discuss a volume as self-evidently significant as the selected poems of a major poet: more pressing because the volume under discussion will become the text and measure of that poet's reputation for a long time; less pressing because the volume's very existence argues convincingly in favor of the poems it contains. So, I don't as much feel either the pressures or the pleasures of advocacy in discussing *Selected Poems* as I did in discussing *A Few Days*. I doubt, for instance, that this generous selection of poems will convert many of Ashbery's professional or amateur detractors. (I have always been grimly amused to note that those who most cry out against Ashbery are those whose minds were made up in advance on the basis of a lazy, self-congratulatory prejudice and therefore are those who have never read him seriously.) This is not a revisionist or conciliatory collection. In it, Ashbery has chosen to represent himself as himself; what is difficult about his poetic nature remains difficult, just as what is sublime in it remains undiminishedly sublime. The other side of the equation should seem then to balance. Those who have long prized Ashbery's work find it easy and in keeping with their own natures to prize this volume.

Yet, there is a third sort of reader I would like to imagine, one perhaps for whom such a volume is best intended: that is, the one who, in this selection, encounters Ashbery seriously for the first time. That reader is at once offered a sense of both the range and the dramatic continuity of Ashbery's venture—a sense that has, in readers like myself, had to develop slowly and, in part, asynchronically. That reader will enjoy an advantageous view of a poet's progress along a distinct path, for, from *Some Trees'* poignant myths of youth and of the imagination's waking into worlds it has and has not made; through the anxious sorting out and recombining of worlds in *The Tennis Court Oath* and *Rivers and Mountains*; into the provisional aesthetic calm of *The Double Dream of Spring* and *Self-Portrait in a Convex Mirror*; and, finally, into the heroic acceptance of endless variousness, of infinite confusion and amazement at what worlds do and can be made to exist from *Houseboat Days* to *A Wave*, it has been Ashbery's long and open purpose to determine just where we might actually be ourselves in the mortal, indistinct shape-shifting country between the objectively and subjectively real. That new reader will experience a perceptual history of self-awareness in this most critically self-aware of times. He, more even than long-devoted followers of Ashbery, may turn out to be Ashbery's ideal judge and advocate. He may share the terrible anticipation of a career lived among the words of poems that Ashbery documents at the close of "The Picture of Little J.A. in a Prospect of Flowers," from the Yale Series volume *Some Trees*:

> Yet I cannot escape the picture
> Of my small self in that bank of flowers:
> My head among the blazing phlox
> Seemed a pale and gigantic fungus.
> I had a hard stare, accepting
>
> Everything, taking nothing,
> As though the rolled-up future might stink
> As loud as stood the sick moment
> The shutter clicked. Though I was wrong,
> Still, as the loveliest feelings

Must soon find words, and these, yes,
Displace them, so I am not wrong
In calling this comic version of myself
The true one. For as change is horror,
Virtue is really stubbornness

And only in the light of lost words
Can we imagine our rewards. (26-42)

The reader who discovers Ashbery in *Selected Poems* may be privileged
to know in the actual context of his own experience the terror of
that shutter's click and of the finality of discovering a true vocation
in seeing poems through the strange country between object and
subject, between the horror of change and the virtue of stubbornness. Likewise, after the journeying of several volumes, he may be
able to share and perhaps to understand as in some way his own
the magnificent resignation to and affirmation of life's contrariety that Ashbery voices in the Orphic masterpiece from *Houseboat
Days*, "Syringa."

. . . But it isn't enough
To just go on singing. Orpheus realized this
And didn't mind so much about his reward being in heaven
After the Bacchantes had torn him apart, driven
Half out of their minds by his music, what it was doing to them.
Some say it was for his treatment of Eurydice.
But probably the music had more to do with it, and
The way music passes, emblematic
Of life and how you cannot isolate a note of it
And say it is good or bad. You must
Wait till it's over. "The end crowns all,"
Meaning also that the "tableau"
Is wrong. For although memories, of a season, for example,
Melt into a single snapshot, one cannot guard, treasure
That stalled moment. It is too flowing, fleeting;
It is a picture of flowing, scenery, though living, mortal,
Over which an abstract action is laid out in blunt,
Harsh strokes. And to ask more than this
Is to become the tossing reeds of that slow,

Powerful stream, the trailing grasses
Playfully tugged at, but to participate in the action
No more than this . . . (27-48)

The rewards imagined at a career's outset remain imagined, as intangible as heaven. The snapshot of little J.A. or of Eurydice captures only a melancholy sense of the fluent, finally ineffable richness of what it cannot capture. To be, by virtue of poems or snapshots, a participant in such fluency is lovely and sufficient to a life, though it is never quite as grand as what the mind can dream up for itself, never quite a long and happy marriage to Eurydice.

In the context of an essay such as this, I can hope only to intimate the emblems and qualities of richness, of various-ness, of courage, candor and the sheer splendor of words as they discover worlds that literally fill Ashbery's *Selected Poems* near to bursting. I can hope only to congratulate those first-time readers I have imagined and to leave them for now with one final instruction. They must never mistake the constant dissatisfaction of Ashbery's speakers, their amazement at the reaches of their own sadness, for either a tragic solipsism or for despair. These speakers find something greater than com-fort in the world's charming and dazzling grace to elude their most ardent, most skilled, most ambitious attempts to include it all in their grand ballades. They find an eternity of barely possible impossibilities, an apparently unlimited sequence of beginnings starting from whatever point they happen to occu-py right now among the strange and familiar décor of their flu-ent mundos.

And you see, both of us were right, though nothing
Has somehow come to nothing; the avatars
Of our conforming to the rules and living
Around the home have made—well, in a sense, "good cit-
izens" of us,
Brushing the teeth and all that, and learning to accept
The charity of the hard moments as they are doled out,
For this is action, this not being sure, this careless
Preparing, sowing the seeds crooked in the furrow,

Making ready to forget, and always coming back
To the mooring of starting out, that day so long ago.
                    ("Soonest Mended" 61-70)

The "charity of the hard moments" is more than charity. It is the guarantee of action and of "grace to be born and live as variously as possible" amidst the storms of contrariety we each endure. It is the great privilege of the readers of Ashbery's *Selected Poems* not only to learn, but to live this best lesson of our time for themselves.

Robert Creeley: The Eventual Victorian

At the climax of Ian McEwan's novel *Saturday*, the main character and his family are held captive in their home by a thug named Baxter. The daughter of the family, Daisy, is a published poet and has been made to strip naked and stand in the center of the room. Baxter then commands her to recite one of her poems to him. In subtle, unnoticed defiance, she recites from memory Matthew Arnold's "Dover Beach."

> . . . Baxter has broken his silence and is saying excitedly, "You wrote that. You *wrote* that."
>
> It's a statement, not a question. Daisy stares at him, waiting.
>
> He says again, "You wrote that." And then, hurriedly. "It's beautiful. You know that, don't you. It's beautiful. And you wrote it."
>
> She dares say nothing.
>
> "It makes me think about where I grew up." (231)

Robert Creeley was a poet of home-places. For him, the phrase "where I'm coming from" was ever explicitly literal and specific. Often, the place to which he referred was one particular poet or one particular poem. Myself, I take deep instruction from the fact that, in the later phase of his writing life, the poem he most often alluded to was "Dover Beach." Strange to say, given its melancholy and stoic resignation, Arnold's masterpiece turns out to be a honeymoon poem, an epithalamion of sorts. Addressed to a beloved, it sorts through desolations in search of tenderness and sweet union. Think, then, of the many desolations of Creeley's early work: the hasting catastrophe of "I Know a Man," the barely contained rage of "The Hill," the gorgeously morbid classicism of

"Heroes." And of course, there is also that most chilling of love poems, "The Warning," which begins:

> For love—I would
> split open your head and put
> a candle in
> behind the eyes. (1-4)

In the later poems comes the great change, not heavy, but lightsome. In those books addressed to his married life with Penelope Highton (whose given name alone speaks volumes and truly did), there is, even in dark moments, unprecedented respite, relief, and ease of tensions. Undeceived but unafraid, mournful but gratefully connected to a common place, a site *in* common, grounded in fidelity and the remembrance of filial piety, Creeley's later work never fails, in any of its occasions, to come all the way home to very first things. The thug, Baxter, in McEwan's novel, avers that "Dover Beach" makes him "think about where (he) grew up." The poet Robert Creeley, in post-lude to the eloquent violence of his early work, likewise references Matthew Arnold's most famous poem as a portal, opening backwards and forward, into peace.

The much-abused notion of "paradigm shift" is nonetheless entirely apt to a true sense of the Victorian imagination. In the backward of warm Christian retrospect and in the forward hopes best characterized by the close of Tennyson's "In Memoriam"—"one far-off divine event, / To which the whole creation moves"—that imagination flourished early in self-confidence and self-assurance. But then the heavy changes disrupted minds and dislodged sureties. Malthus, Marx, and Darwin disturbed all privilege in every direction. "Dover Beach" is the anthem of that disturbance. Both aftermath and prelude, it details a world still very much our own. After an opening stanza of calm and conventional description in which all the tropes of late Romantic landscape poetry are beautifully deployed across the beaches at Dover, Arnold suddenly shifts. First the poem and then the world are seen to change utterly:

Sophocles long ago
Heard it on the Aegean, and it brought
Into his mind the turbid ebb and flow
Of human misery; we
Find also in the sound a thought,
Hearing it by this distant northern sea.

The sea of faith
Was once, too, at the full, and round earth's
      shore
Lay like the folds of a bright girdle furl'd;
But now I only hear
Its melancholy, long, withdrawing roar,
Retreating to the breath
Of the night-wind down the vast edges drear
And naked shingles of the world. (15-28)

Some honeymoon! Backwards goes the poet's mind to a misery predating Christianity: an oceanic misery that proves an implacable precedent. Forward, the poem leans into emptiness. With a shock of sudden insight, "Dover Beach" translates simple landscape into something very much like despair. Somewhere in the space between the poem's conventional opening stanza and the line "Sophocles long ago," we find a perfect synecdoche of the Victorian mind. And too, perhaps, of the experience of every true mind afterwards. The consequence? Despair at first, yes, surely, but then Arnold ventures upon a wild and willed affirmation in full consciousness of despair.

Ah, love, let us be true
To one another! for the world, which seems
To lie before us like a land of dreams,
So various, so beautiful, so new,
Hath really neither joy, nor love, nor light,
Nor certitude, nor peace, nor help for pain;
And we are here as on a darkling plain
Swept with confused alarms of struggle and
      flight,
Where ignorant armies clash by night. (29-37)

Some epithalamion! Yet, this final stanza is perfectly and lovingly undeceived. It proposes a foundation which, albeit desperate, is true. Here, Matthew Arnold finds a model for the marriage of poetry to experience in the aftermath of profound disillusion. Through dire pronouncements, truth somehow manages to embrace another's truth. The name of the embrace is love.

Robert Creeley's first explicit *hommage* to "Dover Beach" appears in his 2003 collection *If I Were Writing This*. The book's title jibes uncannily with the circumstance of McEwan's novel. Daisy survives and, in the process, saves her family via an impersonation, an appropriation of Arnold's poem. Surely, the over-arching theme of Creeley's later work is the project of family life and its projection on to the restless endeavors of our common world. If, by impersonation and loving appropriation, by imagining that he himself were writing "Dover Beach," Creeley might mend and manage the damages that family life inevitably entails, then love could find a way. In this poem "Pictures," dedicated to his wife Penelope, he explores the darkling plains of memory and anxiety just as Arnold does. There is the darkness of the past:

> If one looks back
> or thinks to look
> in that uselessly opaque direction,
> little enough's ever there. (29-32)

In the backward and abysm, "Pictures" shows no help for pain. Opacity obviates imagery and impoverishes the poet's eye. Likewise, futurity is a blindness:

> Like sitting in a back seat,
> can't see what street
> we're on or what the
> one driving sees
> or where we're going.
> Waiting for what's going to happen . . . (74-79)

Beautiful echoes here of "I Know a Man" and also of William Carlos Williams' "No one / to witness / and adjust, no one to drive the car" (*Spring and All*, XVIII 64-66). Yet, between a helpless past and a blinded futurity, Creeley's impersonation of Matthew Arnold bravely and modestly intervenes. The ignorant armies are ignorant surely, and poets despair when simile falls apart in their hands. Nevertheless, reckless faith intervenes.

> I could not compare you to anything.
> You were not like rhubarb
> or clean sheets—or, dear as it might be,
> sudden rain in the street.
>
> All those years ago, on the beach in Dover,
> with that time so ominous,
> and the couple so human,
> pledging their faith to one another,
>
> now again such a time seems here—
> not to fear
> death or what's been so given—
> to yield one's own despair. (62-73)

When the conventions of poetry fail, the poems themselves remain. Discarding simile, "Pictures" reaches out to another poem. Despairing of poetry, Creeley is nevertheless resigned (or as he would himself have said, "given") to the poem at hand. His imagination embraces another imagination, Matthew Arnold's, and faith makes a way. As it turns out, poetry believes in itself. There is a reckless piety of phrasing and phasing here: "now again;" "time seems here." Present and pastness, time and space intertwine, as Creeley comes to realize that love is a bulwark against regret in one direction and despair in another. Gratefully, he "yields" his despair to an acknowledged kinship with a Victorian poet on his honeymoon in Dover.

It is in his last and, sadly, posthumous collection *On Earth* that Creeley makes his affiliation with the Victorian mind most explicit. At the end of his writing life, despair and affirmation become simultaneities. The imagination of "Dover Beach" exclaims a forwardness without the slightest hope for what may lie ahead. Repetitions—the Malthusian and Marxist and Darwinian paradigm—incline toward inevitabilities, prime instances of death and/or disruption. In Creeley's plainsong, these are expressed by his constant recourse to the simple word "Again." So it is that, in *On Earth*, we find "Dover Beach (Again)":

> The waves keep at it,
> Arnold's Aegean Sophocles heard,
> the swell and ebb,
> the cresting and the falling under,
>
> each one particular and the same—
> Each day a reminder, each sun in its world,
>   each face,
> each word something one hears
> or someone once heard. (1-8)

The backward is ever more complex; the poem must reach through Arnold to reach Aegean Sophocles and the primary ebb and flow of human misery. There is an ebb tide in the language and in the human mind. Forward, the poem faces a crowd and wilderness of particulars. Words must somehow be found for each in the absence of any stable definitions. Here is the essence of the Victorian dilemma, and Robert Creeley avows it as his own. Still, there is recourse as Arnold found and as "Dover Beach (Again)" insists in its very first words: "The waves keep at it." Persistence takes the place of pattern and of plan. Persistence and particularity become articles of a new faith accustomed to despair. The tragic passing of every "each" somehow finds its place in a sequence of passages. And so Creeley turns to the elements of his art so as to make an ending. If in the faltering of poetry (and of all its comforting assumptions vis-à-vis canon and continuity) poems continue, then in the faltering of poems, the words themselves, in their solitude, persist. At the end of his writing life, Creeley was a calm and compassionate Lear. Truly an "unaccommodated man," he could despair of poetry while somehow keeping faith with single words. In his last poems, it is easy to hear that the "long, withdrawing roar" is a single word and also to know that such a singularity is sufficient to our needs.

In Robert Creeley's brief essay "Autobiography," there is a sentence utterly striking in its simplicity and avowal. The sentence could pass for an autobiography unto itself.

We believe a world or have none. (Clark 143)

To replace a faith withdrawn into the shadowlands of antiquity, the Victorian mind reached toward a reckless faithfulness: "Ah, love let us be true / to one another!" ("Dover Beach" 29-30) To bridge the gap between despair and affirmation, it imagined an other-worldly worldliness. America's great Victorian, Walt Whitman, called it friendship. Matthew Arnold called it love. In his late work, Creeley folds the two names into one. A faith in the fact of one's relations here and now persists into a credible hereafter. The world as given, in all its contradiction and catastrophe, is nevertheless a world we can believe.

Heaven's Commonplace: *Hoc Opus, Hic Labor Est*

M emories of Robert Creeley are a blessed common ground and meeting place for several generations of American poets—my own especially, as we were fortunate enough to know him first as a teacher and then as a friend. There is a forward congruence to all these memories, an echoic singularity of chastening mischiefs and tender prescience. I step forward here in remembrance now, mindful of one of Bob's most perfect poems, "Heroes," the piece in which the Cumaean Sibyl's injunction to Aeneas at the threshold of the afterlife—"*hoc opus, hic labor est*" —chastens and teases language into filial, eternal return.

Buffalo

In the fall of 1977, I began my graduate studies at the University of Buffalo. On the opening day of term, I walked into Samuel Clemens Hall a little daunted by the prospect of my first class—Modern Poetry with Professor Robert Creeley. I entered the room to find my new classmates seated very quietly, but quietly excited too. We fiddled with the little aluminum foil ashtrays which, in those days, still shone in the top right corner of every desk. When Professor Creeley entered, wearing a fatigue jacket and broad-brimmed hat, his face had a look of surprise and urgency, as though he had just heard some kind of bulletin over the airwaves. He sat on his desk, tilted his head a little and said, "It's like shark repellent." He went on to explain how, in the early days of WWII, the Naval Air Corps had been deeply troubled by the number of planes lost in the Pacific. Fear of shark-infested waters was determined to be a prime cause of pilot error and so, in very short order, pilots were issued newly-devised canisters of shark repellent to be carried on their belts. At this point Creeley laughed a bit, going on to say that the Navy knew the repellent to be ineffective, and yet the stuff went on to have its desired effect. Unafraid, pilots flew with greater confidence and more success. "It's the same with modern poetry." Then Creeley left the room, leaving us with a lesson I've been decades learning. Poetry lives by faith alone, and the work of poetry is always only trust. The least dogmatic poet I ever knew left it there. So we began.

Denver

In 1986, I was an assistant professor in Denver. As ever with the untenured, I was eager to please, to serve, and to prove my mettle. When the public library launched a very posh poetry reading series, I helped to arrange Creeley's visit and to compose the program notes that patrons of the library would find on their front row seats. A few hours before the event there was time for Bob and me to have a quiet dinner. We went to a good place, a Russian restaurant on Larimer Street. Perhaps it was the greeny, home-distilled dill vodka there, or perhaps it was simply the respite from earnest company—in any case, our mood was happy, even a bit silly. I remember us laughing as the butter squirted out of Bob's chicken Kiev all over my tie, and then laughing again as *my* entrée returned the favor. We spoke a lot about Slater Brown, then in his ninetieth year and still enjoying pastries in the cafes of Gloucester and Rockport. Friendship was always Creeley's favorite subject, and of Slater Brown, dear friend of E.E. Cummings and of Hart Crane, he spoke warmly and tenderly indeed. (N.b., Creeley's August 14, 1951, letter to Charles Olson remains, to my mind, the best and most useful close reading of Hart Crane's poetry ever done.) After dinner, we walked to the library and I prepared myself to be public, ceremonious, and posh. Just as we reached the front doors and the well-dressed ticket takers, a beat-up school bus screeched behind us and I heard many voices calling, "Bob, hey

Bob, we made it!" Old friends, old students, old cohorts from the canyons around Boulder. Bob waited for them to park and to join us—there must have been nearly thirty folks in that bus. Then he led them in, pointing to his sudden entourage and saying to the perplexed ticket-takers, "They're with me."

Arden, Nevada

After a busy week of readings and lectures—at the University of Utah, the Decker Lake Reformatory (Bob always had an amazing, calming rapport with angry young men) and the Jewel Box Theater on Flamingo in Las Vegas—Creeley came to spend the weekend at our place in the Spring Mountains. The big issue of our household at the time was the imminence of our son Benjamin's first official haircut. He was four years old, strong-willed then as now, and dead set against it. Bob, keen for peace and relaxation, took Ben aside. They conferred in whispers, and then Bob fetched a towel and scissors. After a very few minutes—no tears, no arguments—Ben was looking dapper and tidy. For several years afterwards, whenever the subject of a haircut would arise, Ben announced proudly: "Only Robert Creeley cuts my hair."

Tuscaloosa

During the spring of the Iraq invasion, I held the post of Coal Royalty Chair in Poetry at the University of Alabama. One of the perks of the job was the chance to invite a major contemporary poet to campus for a reading and colloquium. To no one's surprise and everyone's great pleasure, I invited Bob. His performance, to a packed house in a stately auditorium, was the best I'd ever seen him give. The audience, fretful and edgy from news of the war, had clearly arrived with great and urgent expectations. Bob didn't let them down. He began with a soft-spoken recollection of his own wartime experience in Burma, describing scarifying scenes with characteristic understatement and self-deprecating tact. I could feel all the people around me—scholars and students and outsider artists come to Tuscaloosa from the piney woods—relax into trust, into pleasure. Then Bob read a series of poems about family life and commonplaces, and for an hour there was peace.

Afterwards, there was some sort of mix-up about his hotel, and so Bob came to spend the night in the guest room of the cottage near the Black Warrior River that came with my job. The next morning, after breakfast, I had one of the most serene hours of my entire life. Upstairs, there was a cluster of connected rooms I used for writing—three desks, five comfortable chairs, and more than a dozen little windows looking out into trees already twined with blossoming wisteria. Bob and I lounged up there with our coffee. He caught up on his correspondence and read a while. I typed away at a long poem I'd begun some weeks before. Many birds sang. And then the phone rang. It was the president's office from Brown University, calling for Bob. When he put down the receiver, he looked at me and said, "At my age, it's strange to be starting a new job." By the fall, he'd moved to Providence.

Coda

I never saw Bob again after Tuscaloosa, though we surely kept in touch. In late 2004 I had a bad case of the blues and spent a lot of time sheltering in one of my favorite books, *Kilvert's Diary: 1870–1879*, notes of English curated in a rural parish. One morning, I came to the following passage and could not resist the urge to e-mail it to my friend:

> One bell did not ring loud enough to satisfy the people so they took an axe up to the bell and beat the bell with the axe till they beat it all to pieces.
>
> (Robert Kilvert, *Kilvert's Diary: 1870-1879* 122)

Less than an hour later, Bob replied. His e-mail read: "Just back from visit to not one but two family cemeteries. Small world!" And he attached a new poem:

> One bell wouldn't ring loud enough.
> so they beat the bell to hell, Max,
> with an axe, show it who's boss,
> boss. Me, I dreamt I dwelt in

someplace one could relax
but I was wrong, wrong, *wrong*.
You got a song, man, sing it.
You got a bell, man, ring it.
("Old Story" 1-8)

Robert Creeley died in March of 2005. A few days later, our friend Forrest Gander wrote to me. He'd been putting Bob's office at Brown into order and wanted me to know that the little poem "about Francis Kilvert and the bell" was the last that Bob had ever written. *Hoc opus, hic labor est.*

2

Will Not End: The Expanse of Fragments

All is intact: only fragments can be grasped.

Edmond Jabès, *El, or the Last Book*

Grief exiles us from the habitual, functional intactness of the world. Inconsolable grief declares the permanence of that exile. In poetry, the rituals of form have always served to abrogate exile or, at the very least, to erase its nearest, most hurtful declarations. The completed poem is the consolation of its own origins, and in this sense, every finished poem is an elegy, a successful machine, an apotheosis of habit. In restoring Odysseus to his throne and erasing the foul declarations of the suitors, *The Odyssey* accomplishes an elegiac purpose. In restoring the Grecian Urn to its enigma, rescuing it from the anatomizing insults of perception, Keats' ode is elegiac. And even a poem as exuberant, as self-consecrated to the affirmation of temporality and change as Frank O'Hara's "Biotherm" cannot help but, in its densest imaginable completeness, succeed in rescuing its figures from "mess and measure," thereby closing a shape, withdrawing a security from chaos, practicing elegy. Completeness espouses completion, sometimes joyfully, sometimes grimly, but never uncertainly. What is a scar if not the signature of closure?

Thus, the wound that cannot heal, the grief that cannot or will not accept consolation, can turn only to the fragment as the means of poetic expression uncompromised by any appearance of restoration. A fragment is a poem that never returns the poet to his or her original, unruptured silence, and it is a poem that never finally releases the readers to their functional inattention. The poet continues, as grief continues, to reify the significance of injury and exile by continuing not to finish the poem, understanding and evidencing at one and the same time that to stop is not to conclude. Likewise, the readers continue an alienated, dysfunctional attention to dysfunction as they continue to find no means of escape from the uncertain co-authorship imposed by fragments. Incompleteness is the Elysium of mourning, the wound never to be suppressed by a scar.

> That was different
> My girlhood then
> was in full bloom
> and you—
> > (Sappho)

When Jabès writes that "only fragments can be grasped," he declares the unique *utility* of the fragment. Completeness, being object-ive, mirrors its intact phenomenal precedent, the world. In reading a completed text, we can either accept or reject its version of that precedent, but we are not compelled nor even invited to grasp the text and to use it as the instrument of its own and our own uncertain futurity. Like grief, the fragment places all of its hope, its entire being really, in the undetermined circumstances of the future. Like inconsolable grief, the fragment refuses the backward mimesis of consolation in favor of the unprecedented deformity of its moment and of its featureless next moment.

Sappho remains the primary instigator of the fragment's history and future. It is in the lucid erasure of her partial stanzas that incompleteness is first married to grief and transformed by that marriage into an entirely compelling *text*. In the fragment quoted above, lines speak as lineaments of a pleasure torn apart. Grief inhabits the voided region between then and now, the difference without a name. This difference figures the space between lines one and two, just as the hyphen beyond which there is nothing figures the lost beloved. Time and its changes are not contained and thus accommodated or made commodious by this fragment. The lines are merely the irrefutable evidence of time. Because of time, then and now bear no meaningful resemblance to one another. The beloved, a dear precedent whose only name is "you," is a cause whose effects are endless because they are undescribed. Here Sappho discovers that in the surrender of authority to a hyphen the poet of fragment acquires the freedom to grieve in a syntax as unique and undelineated as the full substance of what has been lost and remains lost.

> Oh! make us
>   suffer
>   you who do not
>   doubt it
> much—all
> that (he) equals
> your life, painful in
>   broken
> us
> ——
>
>   while
>   you glide, free
> (Stéphane Mallarmé, *A Tomb for Anatole* fragment 50, 1-11)

From Symbolism onward, through its various adjuncts and aftermaths, Modernism has embraced the disconsolate with an eerie passion. And so it is among Modern poems that the dismembering Sapphic fragment most fully achieves the status of genre. Certainly, the Romantics were fond of fragments as they were fond of all ruins, genuine or contrived. But this fondness had little to do with grief; rather, it expressed a quality of the egotistical sublime that is the withholding of sacred truths from the uninitiated, the persons from Porlock. It is in modern verse that that fragment reaffirms its marriage to the inconsolable, not in deeply orchestrated mechanisms of *abolie* such as *The Waste Land* and *Mauberley*, but in the heartfelt, uncontrollable resistance to closure enacted in fragments whose purpose is the undistracted endurance of grief's immanence.

Mallarmé's *A Tomb for Anatole*, a series of 202 fragments that beautifully fail to coalesce into a mausoleum for the poet's dead son and fail—at the level of pure syntax—to organize Mallarmé's grief into a distinct, disposable commodity, is the first Modern poem to suffer unprotestingly, without recourse, the music of the inconsolable. As in the Sapphic fragment, the music is of dismemberment. Section fifty (above) well represents the entire series in its consistent rupture of subject from object and of conditions pertaining to grief—such as doubt, such as pain—from their modifiers. Because the lost son survives only in the father's disjunctive suffering, the father must pray for further suffering, further disjunction, if he is to remain any kind of father at all. The son, incommunicado in his impenetrable parentheses, severs the connection between being and life. The disconsolate exist in their grief but cannot live there. The son's death extends this severance to the depth of the monosyllable, to the "us" that, broken now, is no longer plural and whose consequence must be a blank. The disconsolate may speak in the plural, but their condition is permanently singular, void of predicates.

Like Sappho's beloved "you," Anatole escapes the fragment into an absolute indeterminacy, gliding, effortless and free even as his father strives for his own unfreedom in the cause of fidelity to a child who can never now be faithful to him or benefit from his efforts. Here incompleteness liberates the labor of grief from its impure products, from consolation or epitaph. Mallarmé inscribes a syntax wherein the subject, himself, enjoys no influence at all upon its object, Anatole. Thus does his fragment make of mourning an experience more literally immemorial than any tomb.

> M'amour, m'amour
> what do I love and
> where are you?
> That I lost my center
> fighting the world.
> The dreams clash
> and are shattered—

and that I tried to make a paradiso

terrestre.
(Ezra Pound, "Notes for CXVII et seq." 18-26)

Catastrophe and failure prevented Ezra Pound from making a tomb of *The Cantos*, an encyclopedic shrine to the elitist chagrin of his original intention. Pound's Achaians and Dynasts, Malatestas and Blackshirts are absent from his book's end in *Drafts and Fragments*, replaced by a broken, telegraphic shadow whose broken speech is nevertheless Orphic and animated. That a proposed epic should conclude with fragments signals a failure of purpose in favor of reality, in favor of the human limits that grief knows to be, in the direction of pain, limitless. The lover for whom Pound mourns is tragically various, even as she is lexically identical with Sappho's single vanished "you." She is Muse and consensus, authority and community, conviction and craft. In the wreckage of his ideology and of his synthetic re-envisioning of the *Commedia*, Pound makes fragments that, grievingly, affirm the justice of ruin. In the wreckage of his mind and heart after years of imposed and psychically self-imposed confinement, Pound makes fragments that, mournfully, celebrate the victory of the world's inconclusive becoming over his heart's desire to safeguard it and his mind's desire to influence its final shape.

As with Mallarmé, the loss of influence requires a poetic of disempowerment both in form, that is the fragment, and in deep grammar, the syntaxes that evidence the status of the poet in the world. In this fragment, the troubadour's salutation to the Beloved lapses into question and bewilderment. The epic poet's place at the center of a communal history is displaced and the poet marginalized by vain effort. And the dialectic of dreams disintegrates into contentiousness, all because the poet strove to make instead of to be made by the world. Pound's grief is for the loss of a delusory capacity. All the old quantities appear—love and combat and the dream of an enforceable paradise—but again, as with Mallarmé, theirs are the predicates of impotence. Still, Pound never wrote more beautifully or more memorably than here, in his last fragments. Absenting himself via incompleteness, he presents his readers an unmortgaged reality and a human presence speaking without trespass or defacement.

Yet, the absence of trespass and defacement does not restore a broken world; the fragment does not always propose the body of silence as a body of resignation or humility. As there can be combative modes of mourning, there are combative fragments, aggressive silences. In refusing or perpetually deferring consolation, the fragment decries all unbroken forms as forms of torpor. As a means of perceptual expression, the fragment can propound vision as a divorce of the seen from nurturing habits of being, propound fragmentary speech as a divorce of words from their habitual espousal of the integrity of the world.

> It is I who committed suicide one day
> and tore my body from myself
> and battle against what is left of it
> and wish forever to come back to myself
>
> who have founded a false world in the mean time:
> this one
> (Antonin Artaud, "Electroshock Fragments" 135-40)

No poet turns the cruelty of incompletion more combatively against consolation than Artaud. In "Electroshock Fragments," he details ruptures of meaning from meaningfulness and of self from selfhood, comprehending the aphasiac shocks as the spasms of clinical murder they truly are. Here, an abandoned "I," instead of a fleeing Sapphic "you," signifies the crucial absence because it is a selfhood, the very premise of experience, that Artaud mourns. Language is a violence already too remote to be amended, and the effects of language upon consciousness are a dismemberment too thoroughly accomplished to be accessible to grief. There remains only a vain battle against the remains, and a vain wish to return to an annihilated point of origin. Pound's fragments dismember the epic intention of restoration in the name of a benign process. Artaud's fragments dismember the neutral body of that intention in the name of a gratuitous violence: grief as an *acte gratuite*. Consolation, like epic, represents the foundation of a possible future. Artaud's spasmodic fragments expose the unreality of the real, the falsity of "this" world, obviating all futures. So, the moment of aphasia consumes eternity, and speech mourns the speaker with a limitlessly deprived fidelity.

Before My

>   sheetlightning knee
>   the hand comes to rest,
>   with which you
>   drove over the eye,
>   a clinking
>   attains certitude
>   in the circle I drew
>   around us both,
>   sometimes however
>   heaven dies
>   before
>   our fragments.
>
> (Paul Celan, "Before My" 1-12)

From extremes of humility to extremes of aggression, the inconsolable fragment vocalizes a state in which time and silence are the continuous media of being—media scarred by grief and speech, but nonetheless continuous. The completed poem, the accomplished elegiac rite, testifies on behalf of an intact community of speakers, a closed wound. Its testimony identifies the forms of experience as recurrent, quantifiable events, claiming for itself a place among those forms, one quality of which is the authority to console. The fragment, the accomplished open wound of silence, testifies to the rupture of a solitary voice from the media which had concealed its solitude. Its testimony identifies experience as the antithesis of form, claiming for itself a suitably antithetical place whose authority is an endless act of surrender to the instant of grief.

No event of Modernity is more justly inconsolable than the Holocaust. If such an event can have a poet, he is Paul

Celan; and if Celan can be said to excel in a specific genre, it is in the genre of fragments brought to their purest and most harrowing authority. Moving away from the elegant elegiac symmetries of early poems such as his much anthologized "Death Fugue," Celan spoke more and more in the syntax of rupture. His sentences chose rims and precipices for their subjects, and the inconsolable verbs—to love, to speak, to contact—cast themselves down. By the time he was composing the dense fragments collected posthumously in *Zeitgehoft*, he had discovered inchoate genocide in isolate syllables, fierce inclinations to closure that he resisted by means of deformed and deforming silences. The certitude inside of a drawn circle, like the citizenry of heaven, is death. The consolations of form and completeness require death as their antecedent. To protest the Holocaust in grief's name, Celan abandons elegance. His words escape their sentences, and his fragments survive heaven because they somehow find the means to resist their deepest, dearest imperatives toward conclusion. Inconsolable grief cannot be reconciled to order. The fragment, in the grammars and demystifying mysteries of incompleteness, disorders the final solutions of poetry into the real time and real silence of mourning.

Without a Golden Age: Genre in Diaspora

When accepted, the consolations of genre provide continuity, offering poets the sympathetic attention and collaboration of official history. To accept genre is to accept a canon and the canon's promise that its formulae will succeed: the elegy will console, the satire chasten, the ode praise. The providence of genre grants poets access to a ready-made consensus that they address by orchestrating the particulars of their experience according to the pre-set patterns of canon. Yet, as the climate of our time has proven more and more hostile to consensus, poets have found or been compelled to seek other uses for genre, other accommodations with form. Each failure or rejection of genre summons originality and improvisation. When history proves useless and consensus chimerical, the poet's necessity is invention, and this does a lot to explain our day's preference for revision over mimesis. The strengths of the poems made (as well as of those rediscovered and praised) in the past ninety years or so exercise the pressures of revision: the reconfiguration of elegy towards the inconsolable, the resignation of satire to history's incorrigibility, the lamentation of odes that grieve in anticipation of the absence of the objects of their praise. In just this way, the formal decorums of poetry, the arithmetic elaborations of song meter divorced from music by the printed page, serve the revisionist poet as masks of indeterminacy and vehicles of irrationality despite the reassurances of repetition and rhyme; pantoums assert the randomness of syntactical meaning, sestinas transform closure into a musical toy, and so on. Demystified by the inutility and inversion of genre, such patterns deconstruct themselves through the very precision of their performance, much as the grids in a Dieben-korn painting disappear into the asymmetrical inexpressive-ness of the beautiful canvas as a whole. But form follows genre as method follows need, and it is with the loveliness of genre's necessary, nonce revisions that I am most concerned here.

The traditional canons of genre point backwards to-ward a still center, a Golden Age in which perception and rep-resentation, experience and the poem about experience, are somehow congruent. By orienting themselves in relation to this center, traditionalist poets adopt the gestures of canon in expectation of canonical success. Genre "works" when this success takes the form of transparency in style and universali-ty in expression. Yet, the poet who, for whatever reason, can-not credit a Golden Age or feel in touch with one, does not an-ticipate such forms of success. For such a poet, genre is a pres-sure to be resisted or redirected by the imperatives of every in-dividual poem. Wallace Stevens asserts this in as early a piece as "Anecdote of the Jar."

> I placed a jar in Tennessee,
> And round it was, upon a hill.
> It made the slovenly wilderness
> Surround that hill.
>
> The wilderness rose up to it,
> And sprawled around, no longer wild.
> The jar was round upon the ground
> And tall and of a port in air.
>
> It took dominion everywhere.
> The jar was gray and bare.
> It did not give of bird or bush,
> Like nothing else in Tennessee. (1-12)

Centeredness here depends not upon a Golden Age, but upon an improvisation, the placing of a common object in an actual landscape. The improvisation does not pretend to have dis-covered a center, but frankly, even arbitrarily, to have made one. This center works simply because the speaker's perception credits it. It cannot be represented or claim universality. The jar's dominion, the genre of *this* anecdote, is provisional. Only this particular poem can recreate this gesture. Exemplary but unprescriptive, "Anecdote of the Jar" simultaneously affirms both the power and the pluralism of centeredness.

But Stevens, convinced as he is of the Emersonian self-reliance of indeterminacy, of the poem's power to invent, to believe, and, in believing, validate a center of its own, discovers only half of the process by which improvisation re-envisions genre. Perhaps his lifelong desire for accustomedness prevented his acknowledging that the improvised center of a poem itself moves within the poem. The jar travels beyond Tennessee, companioning the poet's perception of a possible aesthetic universal (the "port in air") even as it drifts backwards, away from the poet into the unchanging Tennessee of the representational page. The new uses of genre are not merely alternative readings, the substitution of personal utility for the ventriloquism of a Golden Age. The revisions I have in mind reanimate traditional form, restoring freedom (and thus uncertainty) to poetic gesture. In his "Ode," Valery Larbaud exemplifies this in the figure of a railway train. Here, the poem's enthusiasm is not directed towards the central figure, as would be the case in a conventional ode. Rather, the train is *used* as a vehicle towards the inexpressible. Larbaud wants to appropriate some of the qualities of train-ness for the impulsion of his imagination into indeterminacy:

> Lend me, O Orient Express, Sub-Brenner-Bahn, lend me
> Your miraculous deep tones and
> Your vibrant string-voices;
> Lend me the light, easy respiration
> Of your high, thin locomotives with their graceful
> Movement, the express engines
> Drawing effortlessly four yellow gold-lettered carriages
> Through the mountain solitudes of Serbia,
> And farther on, through rose-heaped Bulgaria...
>
> Ah, these sounds and this movement
> Must enter into my poems and express

For me my inexpressible life,
The life of a child whose only desire
Is to hope eternally for airy, distant things. (20-33)

The object serves the poem, not the poem the object. Larbaud pursues not the train but the unexpressed desire whose Golden Age is yet to come, if it comes at all. His revision of the ode reifies eternity, not the eternal. Only the future suffices.

As genre is accepted as the organic nature of poetry, so canons are natural histories. Mimesis privileges the nature of what is, subordinating the future to what the present receives from the past and perpetuates through repetition. The mimetic canon is a hall of mirrors, a natural history of limitless recession. It grants poets the authority to compose variations on the theme "whatever is, is right" and to propound the visible nature of the world as the indisputable source of that authority. Thus, poets as seemingly antithetical as Pope and Coleridge can be accommodated by the same canon, as each avers the complete sufficiency of his moment as a text of what is true. Revisionism, under the impulse of indeterminacy, privileges the undelineated nature of what *might* be or what must be summoned into being by the crisis of immanence. It subordinates the past to what the future unsystematically salvages from that past, and what is salvaged is reconfigured without respect for its original forms in order that it may be put to use in the needful improvisations of new poems. A grand example of such reconfiguring is Frank O'Hara's "Meditations in an Emergency," a poem made up of prose statements that, abandoning the meditation's traditional purpose of arriving at a new knowledge of reality through achieving a perfect understanding of or identity with a particular place or object, frantically disassembles all the pre-texts of the poet's literal being in order to accomplish an escape rather than an arrival. The poem's central paragraph well represents the whole:

My eyes are vague blue, like the sky, and change all the time; they are indiscriminate but fleeting, entirely specific and disloyal, so that no one trusts me. I am always looking away. Or again at something after it

has given me up. It makes me restless and that makes
me unhappy, but I cannot keep them still. If only I had
grey, green, black, brown, yellow eyes; I would stay
at home and do something. It's not that I'm curious.
On the contrary, I am bored but it's my duty to be
attentive, I am needed by things as the sky must be
above the earth. And lately, so great has *their* anxiety
become, I can spare myself little sleep. (17-25)

"Meditations in an Emergency" takes its place in a revisionist
canon, a natural history of boundless mutability wherein authority is congruent with invention and poets (in the process of
composition) discover the authority to aver "whatever is, is not
enough." In such a history, visible nature is disrupted and orig-
inals sought in futurity, in action. This canon does not reject
the past; it views it as an impetus, not as a model. It purposes to
have other purposes than those intended by genre.

All poems originate in disruption. The substance of a
poem, together with its form, describes an elaboration of anxiety towards restoration (Classicism), reconciliation (Romanticism), or renunciation of the ethos that ordains that such-
and-such an event is disruptive rather than normative. This
third elaboration is the response of revision in poetry. As
death, the fundamental disruption of the individual universe,
sets the pattern for all other disruptions, so elegy is, I think,
the best genre to examine first. Our century's radical changes
of what elegies propose and accomplish under the unambiguous pressures of grief serve as intense paradigms for the changes wrought in other, subtler and less urgent genres such as the
satire and the ode.

"For the Union Dead" is a watershed poem not only in
the context of Robert Lowell's career, but in the career of lyric verse in English. The poem gathers several modes of grief—
personal, civic, and historical—into a diction remarkable for
being both sculptural (appropriating the manner of its central
image, the St. Gaudens' relief) and conversational throughout
its seventeen irregular quatrains. The poem's ultimate emotional effect accumulates indirectly, originating in a fairly con-

ventional elegiac gesture. The poet discovers an emblem of time's depredations—the defunct aquarium—that summons a memory of childhood.

> The old South Boston Aquarium stands
> in a Sahara of snow now. Its broken windows are boarded.
> The bronze weathervane cod has lost half its scales.
> The airy tanks are dry.
>
> Once my nose crawled like a snail on the glass;
> my hand tingled
> to burst the bubbles
> drifting from the noses of the cowed, compliant fish.
>
> ("For the Union Dead," 1-8)

What is lost is time and an early sense of wonder at nature's works. The reader feels well prepared at this point for a standard neo-romantic elegy whose purpose, he expects, will be to recapture a sense of wonder in nature's persistence, thus restoring his faith in time's benevolence. However, this expectation is wonderfully surprised as the poem deflects the speaker's emotion away from his present sadness and self onto the violated surface of the Boston Common dug up to make space for an underground garage. Within *this* scene, the poem encounters a literal synecdoche of the violation of both the place and its Puritan ideality: the St. Gaudens' relief. The sculpture is a monumental irony that "sticks like a fishbone / in the city's throat" (Lowell 29-30) as the slaughter of Colonel Shaw's black regiment resonates with all subsequent events that have belied the ideality that sent them to their useless deaths: the victory that achieved freedom in name only for our nation's black people; the self-congratulatory abstraction of brutal civil war into statues that "grow slimmer and younger each year"; the obscenity of Hiroshima and total warfare; and finally, the coming extension of the commerce of imperialism into outer space. Rapidly and immitigably, "For the Union Dead" traduces its original elegiac nostalgia in favor of outrage at a historical infamy whose roots may be found in the deludedness of such nostalgia. Beside Boston's mendacious monuments to its own righteousness can be found more telling emblems: the defunct aquarium, the gouged Common, the Boylston Street window display that uses a photo of Hiroshima to advertise a safe. Instead of consolation, the poem drives towards an intensification of pain through proliferation.

> Colonel Shaw
> is riding on his bubble,
> he waits
> for the blessed break.
>
> The Aquarium is gone. Everywhere,
> giant finned cars nose forward like fish;
> a savage servility
> slides by on grease.
>
> (Lowell 61-68)

Elegy is re-envisioned as the universalization of a private acedia. The poet's environment is as disconsolate as he, and the pathetic fallacy that once was a provisional means of elegy is now its end. Perhaps that is what becomes of all genres in our time; unwilling to subordinate themselves to bankrupt idealities, means resist and ultimately overwhelm ends.

Yet, the overwhelmings are continuous and various. The disconsolate elegy has thrived and diversified since the appearance of "For the Union Dead," as revision has proven itself to possess as many means and occasions to revise as canonical genres possess precedents to cite. Distinctive as their methods and vocabularies are, poems such as Strand's "Elegy for My Father" and Tate's "The Lost Pilot" participate in a discrete and recognizable counter-tradition of poems that improvise an unrestorative but authentic music out of grief, music no less accessible for its being improvised. Quite recently, this counter-tradition has been evidenced in Bin Ramke's *The Erotic Light of Gardens*, a collection whose poems reach into the media of painting and televised history to set new icons in motion to the music of revision. The book's strongest poem, "Elegy as Origin," concludes:

Listen, you who are old enough to remember:
when Eichmann was tried in his glass booth,
did he look separate, apart from us?
Was there air in that box, the same as ours?

You know those international conferences,
when men and women in glass boxes talk into their fists,
their microphones, the simultaneous translators breathing
the air of Paris in New York, of Moscow in Chile?

Or the paintings of Francis Bacon, the red Pope
purifying in his square glass cage like Superman
changing clothes, shuffling his mortal coil
to emerge naked as an emperor talking
all languages, confessing to everything,
to every Jew and Gentile, dying like he meant it, naked.
    (113-126)

Ramke hints at a revisionist anti-community whose improvisations and ghostly translations deepen even as they proliferate in response to the naked anonymity of factual death. Genre propounds the homogeneity of history. Revision, with its perpetual motto *Es Könnte Auch Anders Sein*, propounds the polyglot, the pluralistic, the inconclusively human.

    Under the inconstant aegis of pluralism, other genres follow the elegy into emergency and revision. Indeed, the atmospheres of many poems and entire collections seem charged with a sense of emergency-in-advance, a more than strong suspicion that when the disruptive subject/occasion arrives, the poet will have to makeshift from the very start, inadequately equipped by a canon whose prescriptions are as unhelpful as they are elegant. This suspicion leads, for example, to a distinctive kind of opening gambit in poems—a gesture which, as it initiates the poem's response to disruption, also protects the makeshifting poet momentarily, allowing him or her a brief space in which to prepare for the improvising ahead. Such memorable tropes as the opening of Ashbery's "Self-Portrait in a Convex Mirror" ["As Parmigianino did it, the right hand / Bigger than the head, thrust at the viewer /And swerving easily away, as though to protect / What it advertises . . ."(1-4)] and of Hass's "Meditation at Lagunitas" ["All the new thinking is about loss. / In this it resembles all the old thinking." (1-2)] are gestures of authority made in the absence of authority and afford poets the necessary, if fictive stature they need in order to win the reader's trust until such time as the sincerity and courage of the poem's improvisations can lay a more authentic hold upon it.

Of all the genres, none is more directly involved with authority and trust than satire. Conceived as the articulation of rebuke and as the delineation of correction, the satire traditionally assumes the viability of a common ethos, a set of principles which, when superimposed upon the delinquent present, reveals and banishes all deviations from its stately, transparent ideal. Vice and folly are exposed to contempt in being excluded from the undifferentiated pattern of the just. Citizens of vastly different communities, Juvenal, Pope, and all traditional satirists in whatever century equate aberration with vice and any sense of ultimate apart-ness with folly. The precariousness of satire in our own time is easy to imagine, as our poets more often than not root their work in purposefully aberrant points of view and in the ideal of heroic apart-ness bequeathed them by Romanticism. The tension and the sad beauty of contemporary satire arise from a nostalgia for community experienced even as the poet comes to understand that community is a desperate fiction capable of great viciousness in the defense of its folly against the witness of individuality. Yearning for transparency, our satirists end up exposing themselves to even further isolation by identifying with the eccentric and pariah who cannot long endure the malice of outraged social fictions. Our satirists conclude that the world is incorrigible by virtue of just those motives that made it seem perfectible to earlier poets. Their gestures are defensive rather than corrective, their ethics jagged with human contrariness, never transparent.

A lovely exemplar of contemporary satire is Robert Hass's "Against Botticelli," a poem that, in seeking continuity along the *via negativa* of negation and of our common impov-

erishments, disproves the notion that doubled negatives pro-
duce a positive. Hass prepares his case against the painter before turning to his paintings. Yet, deconstruction in the absence of a subject results only in self-annihilation, the discon-
tinuation of discontinuity.

> In the life we lead together every paradise is lost.
> Nothing could be easier: summer gathers new leaves
> to casual darkness. So few things we need to know.
> And the old wisdoms shudder in us and grow slack.
> Like renunciation. Like the melancholy beauty
> of giving it all up. Like walking steadfast
> in the rhythms, winter light and summer dark.
> And the time for cutting furrows and the dance.
> Mad seed. Death waits it out. It waits us out,
> the sleek incandescent saints, earthly and prayerful.
> In our modesty. In our shamefast and steady attention
> to the ceremony, its preparation, the formal hovering
> of pleasure which falls like the rain we pray not to get
> and are glad for and drown in . . . (1-14)

The improvised ceremony fails as surely as those inherited
from posterity. Abnegation prepares us to see nothing, and
the case against Botticelli only affirms his unassailable stat-
ure. As Hass continues, "we are not even in the painting by
Bosch / where the people are standing around and looking at
the frame / of the Botticelli painting."(19-21) In our culture,
candor is aberrant and must affirm the beautiful aberrance
of art. Thus, the poem's second and final movement happens
upon its true praise of Botticelli in the future of a pair of lovers
making a socially aberrant sort of love, rejecting the canonical
mythos which

> . . . is different in kind from a man and the pale woman
> he fucks in the ass underneath the stars
> because it is summer and they are full of longing
> and sick of birth. They burn coolly
> like phosphorus, and the thing need be done
> only once. Like the sacking of Troy

it survives in imagination,
in the longing brought perfectly to closing,
the woman's white hands opening, opening,
and the man churning inside her, thrashing there.
And light travels as if all the stars they were under
exploded centuries ago and they are resting now, glowing.
The woman thinks what she is feeling is like the dark
and utterly complete. The man is past sadness,
though his eyes are wet. He is learning about gratitude,
how final it is, as if the grace in Botticelli's *Primavera*,
the one with sad eyes who represents pleasure,
had a canvas to herself, entirely to herself. (35-52)

Aberration educates and illuminates aberration. The lovers—
infecund, not face to face but alone—are isolated in the seasons,
and their keen self-consciousness grants them eyes to see "the
grace in Botticelli's *Primavera*" should they need or wish to do
so. Hass's satire rejects ethical community in favor of the terror
that isolated hearts gratefully acknowledge as the subjectively
beautiful, the aesthetic that may fix upon a particular (*e.g.*, the
sad-eyed grace) and elevate it to the level of a universal.

    While other revisionist satires may not capitulate to
their subjects, lauding the freakishness canon urges them to
decry, with quite the same tensely dramatic gestures employed
by Hass, they do surprise their readers with praise and with
their language's final affiliation with the aberrant, the unlike,
the isolate. Poems such as Bishop's "The Man-Moth" and Hu-
go's "A Snapshot of the Auxiliary" discover new forms of tenderness, not by pitying their respective monsters but by swear-
ing helpless, unregretted allegiance to them. Thus, tenderness transforms the genre of rebuke into one of love. Satire becomes epithalamion. A more recent occurrence of this transformation takes place in Ashbery's "Vaucanson" from *April Gal-
leons*. Renowned in the eighteenth century as a maker of autom-
atons (most notably of a mechanical duck that performed vir-
tually all the functions of the natural thing), Vaucanson would
seem an ideal target for twentieth-century satire, a man whose
clockwork vision of things patently offends the holistic relativ-

ism of our time. Yet, in "Vaucanson," Ashbery quickly moves beyond natural commonplaces, discovering a "kinship" with the elaborate toymaker in their mutual desire to revise, to make a place for human invention within the generic *fait accompli* of nature. Ashbery concludes:

> Sinews are loosened then,
> The mind begins to think good thoughts.
> Ah, this sun must be good:
> It's warming again,
> Doing a number, completing its trilogy.
> Life must be back there. You hid it
> So no one would find it
> And now you can't remember where.
>
> But if one were to invent being a child again
> It might just come close enough to being a living relic
> To save this thing, save it from embarrassment
> By ringing down the curtain,
>
> And for a few seconds no one would notice.
> The ending would seem perfect.
> No feelings to dismay,
> No tragic sleep to wake from in a fit
> Of passionate guilt, only the warm sunlight
> That slides easily down shoulders
> To the soft, melting heart. (21-39)

Invention, however short-lived or embarrassing, is the creature of a tragic passion Ashbery refuses to defame. If the resistance to genre is hopeless, Ashbery chooses to celebrate the pathos of that hopelessness, its "soft, melting heart," rather than to distance himself from its folly. As the revision of elegy denies homogeneity, such revision of satire denies hierarchy, leveling the ethical to a borderless plain of sympathies and heartbreaking distances.

    Still, our time's twinned processes of revision and denial have more often seized upon the ode than upon any other genre, perhaps because the ode, even in its most classical formats, is so supple and multifarious, more a tone (formal and laudatory) than a pattern. One could almost write a history of modern poetry simply by charting its periodic recourse to the ode, noting such bold deviations as these: the paralytic irony of Ransom's "The Equilibrists" that makes the form into a frieze; the rhyming conversationalism of Moore's "To a Giraffe" that retunes the ode into personal absolution; the remarkable Pindarics (faithfully comprised of strophe, antistrophe, and epode as Marjorie Perloff has detailed) of O'Hara's "Ode to Willem de Kooning" in which Pindar's triumphal motives are supplanted by those of the isolation and injury suffered by artists in a democracy of "stunning collapsible savages." But *because* of its suppleness, the ode seems able to accommodate these deviations and to remain itself still, retaining the canonical authority of utility. Only quite recently, in poems that bring enormous pressure to bear upon the very notion of praise between subject and object, has the ode been revised to the point of denial. Such pressure abbreviates the ode's usual stately progress in favor of a farewell gesture to what is too transient to join, too quickly disappearing to accept praise.

In "To a Stranger (at the End of a Caboose)," Laura Jensen's speaker is so intensely aware of both the complexity of her subject's unknown life and of her own reflexive poetic motive (*i.e.*, the urge to escape into otherness via language) that her ode becomes a circle of absence whose perimeter is a speeding train wheel and whose center is regretful "afterthoughts."

> There is a sway that comes soon after
> a question. Oatheart, riding a train
> in another language, turns from tense
> to tense around a verb wheel, its maze
> and answer like an angel that missed Adam
> and followed like a leaf into traffic.
>
> Summer was a boxcar, never abandoned,
> never reclaimed. Summer was unsteady
> in detail. He had coveted the thistles
> from Rock Island to the Reading,
> and seen from a train vitality;
> there's more to a farm than patience.

But here are the children side by side
apart from the arty barren farmhouse, really
traveling with the weight of the stack
of their pumpkins, each hauled from the vine
like a suitcase or a sack of money.

In the inner wheel of Oatheart's head
they are traveling farther than the road
from the world in their winter backdrop;
traveling themselves, why not? Changed
by the train wheel, and by afterthoughts. (1-22)

Questions disappear, not into answers, but into mazes of unknown language. Summer disappears into thistles. Children
simply disappear. As all things are "traveling themselves," none
delays long enough to accommodate the poet's desire to borrow its otherness for a moment of relief. Jensen revises the
ode through candor, through allowing all her poem's objects
an impetus of desire as strong and as swift as her own. And by
means of this candor, she denies herself that vivid, albeit fictive, instant in which praise becomes identity with the object of
praise, that instant from which conventional odes draw their
primary satisfaction. Here, where revisionary denial becomes
self-denial, indeterminacy touches upon the heroic.

It is heroism (in minor keys, in the studious gestures
of disillusionment) that continues to fill circles of absence with
new poems. All distances imply death, as every object that re-
cedes from sight implies an ultimate abandonment. With this
in mind, it is beautiful to see Brenda Hillman conclude her
book *Fortress* with the ode "To the Gull." The title participates in
the conventional, preparing us for stanzas in praise of a creature of the air. But very quickly, the poem makes use of another
meaning of "gull," *i.e.*, a victim of deception, a dupe.

Does a poem pre-exist
as dawn pre-exists,
as the dagger smelt shine
before being caught,
taking breath into finality?

You wait nearby
with the curved, resentful
nose of medieval peasantry,
your still, disinterested eye
coming straight from the mind
of Dürer . . . (1-11)

Genre is illusion, a confidence trick of history that seeks to blur the distinction between the processes of nature ("dawn") and the indeterminate, speculative activities of imagination ("poem"). The one cannot contain or disappear into the other; to believe otherwise is to populate both the world and the page with unviable grotesques. The gull is real; Dürer's drawings are real. Yet, their simultaneous existence, like that of perception and desire, does not imply union or even intersection. The yearning for absolute freedom inspired by a bird in flight achieves liberation for neither poet nor gull. In the end, there are no reliable emblems. Each thing, each response lives alone in its integrity. And this integrity applies to desire, the poem's urge to quiet the disruption that is its origin. Hillman concludes:

Oh, take me too!
Over the tortured cypresses,
over the freighters stopped like words,
for the spell is broken
and the muse is dead,
do you see his body
on the battered sloop?
Why are you
at the rail again, kelp
caught in your claw, tracing
with your poet's eye another
blinding circle you must fill? (39-50)

In Hillmans's re-envisioning, the ode is a "blinding circle" whose circumference is the hard outline and limit of integrity and whose center is the black pupil of death into which illusion, perception, and imagination struggle singly not to collapse.

What this re-envisioning denies is the very existence of canon in any useful sense: "The muse is dead." Each poem is alone, striving to replace absences with words so as not to dwell too long on the absences that *are* words. Divorced from consensus, aware of the arbitrariness of even its most elemental signifiers (no word for "gull" has wings; no word for "Paradise" calls immortality out of the fact of death), each poem is at liberty in the ruins of every genre: elegiac in that it begins in loss; satiric in that its corrective urge, however deflected, explains its sympathies; odic in that its desire for otherness outlines the form in which it is finally abandoned or resolved. This is the liberty that Adam and Eve met outside the Garden. Both unrestricted and unconsoled by history, this liberty is the indeterminacy out of which every poem now fashions the determination of its lonely, complete statement, its complete thought.

Betraying the Silence

All closure is repression, the miscarriage of consequence by form, and so a poet's role in the new millennium is to oppose the sense of an ending with a sense of origins, to resist closure with the force of anticipation and the forming ideology of the coming century. I have a name for this ideology, I hope an unrestrictive one. I call it "nextness." Prior to anything else, an artist's work is consecrated to nextness. A composer's immediate being orients itself towards the next note. As a poet, I must incline my entire presence towards the next word. Any distraction defames the reality of time and subordinates it to the vapidities of repetition. To be endurable, our day or any day must be made wholly of next moments, of an integrity unaccommodated by closure, unreconciled to pretty variations.

The next betrays the past, refusing the humble status of aftermath. The next deprivileges the past, voiding its sense of climax. The next adjourns the past, dispersing its shadow community into unincorporated futures. Its technique is disloyalty. Its rationale begins by comprehending the virtue of the betrayals it must betray in its turn.

In an address given at the University of Hamburg in 1969, Graham Greene espoused the technique of disloyalty as crucial to a writer's survival and usefulness, to a writer's *momentum*.

> Loyalty confines you to accepted opinions . . . but disloyalty encourages you to roam through any human mind. . . .

I must be ready to roam into my next mind if I am to write my next poem, the poem that will betray my present mind and the poem I finished yesterday. To accept any opinion, even my own, would make the next poem impossible. To accept the turn of century as the end of anything would be to conspire at the still-birth of the years ahead. To accept the complete satisfactoriness of any thought or word would mute the next word, as surely as our poor decade's obsession with love's hygiene has muted its forlorn, refractive passion. There is a better hygiene, and more compassionate one. Greene concluded his discourse on the technique of disloyalty with this aspiration:

> If only writers would maintain that one virtue of disloyalty—so much more important than chastity—unspotted from the world.

Disloyalty is chaste because it refuses to surrender even the least fragment of possibility to experience. Neither poems nor centuries are the creations of erosion. They are creatures of proliferation, of a nextness that will not wait for the permission of either forms or agendas; a nextness whose perfections remain unabducted by any idea of mine or yours or by anyone's idea of us.

To betray is not to end or to complete. It is to liberate the futurity confined by the thing betrayed. It credits time with absolute reality by discrediting the absolute. At the center of the last century, a large sound of many sounds dominated our languages and the transactions of those languages. The sound was of utopian ideologies. As the Cult of the Virgin (to use Auden's trope) yielded to the Cult of the Dynamo, the manifestoes proliferated with tireless éclat. And in that proliferation, in all that noise, the unspeakable methodically transpired in camps and side-streets, in ditches and firestorms, and millions of individual voices drowned in loud announcements of New Heaven and New Earth. So, it is not at all surprising that those artists who were not consumed by cannibal utopias turned themselves and their residual hearts towards silence. When language becomes mass murder, the ethos evolved by Karl Kraus in response to the horrors of World War I seems the only just poetic: "Let him who has something to say step forward and be silent." When the human becomes the vehicle of mass murder, the project of Marcel Duchamp—the "dehumanization of art via readymades"—seems the artist's only just purpose.

The greatest literary imaginations of the mid-century strove to betray murderous utopian noises by means of silence. Their resistance, their testimony, their judgment, and their vengeance were all enacted by their refusal to say one word more than was completely true or absolutely unrestrainable. The greatest literary imaginations of the mid-century strove to unbuild the busy utopian murderer by re-envisioning human character as its smallest possible gesture, its stillest, most isolated destiny. They rescued what is most essentially human by reducing it to something so elemental that it could not be corrupted save by utter destruction. Thus, of all the central poets of that era—Popa, Parra, Mandelstam, Char, and Celan—it is Paul Celan, the martyr of silences, who matters most.

Cello Entry

from behind pain:
the powers, graded
towards counter-heavens
roll out indecipherable things
in front of arrival runway and drive,

the
climbed evening
is thick with lung-scrub,
two
smoke-clouds of breath
dig in the book
which the temple-din opened,

something grows true,

twelve times the
beyond hit by arrows lights up,

the black-
blooded woman drinks
the black-blooded man's semen,

all things are less than
they are,
all are more.

(Celan, "CELLO ENTRY 1-20)

Or:

HOW YOU die out in me:
down to the last
worn-out
knot of breath
you're there, with a
splinter
of life.

(Celan, "HOW YOU" 1-7)

The more from the less, the splinter of life salvaged from the
shipwreck of life, justifies Celan and rejustifies poetry from inside of a history from which the poet himself could not, in the
end, be rescued. Likewise, among those who reinvented the nature of human character in language at midcentury—Böll, Rob-
be-Grillet, Beckett—it is Samuel Beckett whose urgent silence
most crucially elaborates the just minims of a viable humanity.

> The memory came faint and cold of the story I might
> have told, a story in the likeness of my life, I mean
> without the courage to end or the strength to go on.
> (Beckett, "The End" 72)

Or:

> And were there one day to be here, where there are
> no days, which is no place, born of the impossible
> voice and the unmakable being, and a gleam of light,
> still all would be silent and empty and dark, as now,
> as soon now, when all will be ended, all said, it says,
> it murmurs.

(Beckett, *Texts for Nothing* 140)

The story that *might* have been told is the uncorrupted story, the future that remains possible. The murmur out of silence is the original frequency of the entirely, essentially real—broadcasting nothing and thereby continuing the uncorrupted merely human. The silences of Celan and Beckett are not conceived to solace the survivors of utopia. They are meant to survive the survivors, and in so doing they accomplish a generosity to posterity that is the best motive of any resistance. The utopians bequeathed us an empty din and mountains of corpses. The silences bequeathed us the possibility of ourselves as the beginnings of something truthful to be said.

Our practice, now, and our study ought to find means of writing beyond those beginnings. The benefit of silence is the cleanliness it affords to the sounds that follow it. Silence prepares and fills the hall so that the music may begin unimpeded by the distractions of precedent. Sadly, the silences of Beckett and Celan and their contemporaries have been so misread, so misused by most of the writers of my generation that silence has deteriorated into mere reticence. Out of Beckett, we have made a minimalism in which character is little more than an integer of victimization. Out of Celan, we have fashioned the modest, liberal witness of lyric poems in which experience is seldom more than a parable of uncertainty, poems in which perception is an event to be endured rather than extended to farther reaches of language, to deep grammars in which there are no victims but only new syllables accompanying perception into new meanings. An opportunity has been squandered. By meekly keeping faith with a misinterpreted silence, by revering it instead of betraying it into use, my generation has nearly reduced the struggles of our predecessors to incidents of diminishment, nearly degraded our new millennium to the status of a hapless diminuendo. The laconic terseness of the minimalists reclaims no authority, anticipates no future. The polite reflections of our lyrics revive no major harmonies, assert few new tones. Self-muted, our moment haunts itself.

To honor our reality and that of the writers who prepared it, we must betray the silence, and in our vocable nextness recapture the large character, the large word, perhaps even the large purposes of the utopian itself, on behalf of those humane purposes which, though preserved by silence, many only be fulfilled by the most expansive sentences of which humanity is capable. Having survived, fiction and poetry must once again presume to live, and in so doing, declare exactly what it means to live. Such authority requires the revival of the grand gesture, the didactic example. And the grand gesture requires a profligacy with words in which there is no place for either reticence or modesty. As Williams wrote in *Paterson*:

> Only one answer: write carelessly so that nothing
> that is not green will survive. (155)

As writers and readers, *we* are the greenness now budding out of the silences of the last century. Our success depends upon our betrayal of the careful measures of our forebears by means of a liberated and liberating wantonness with the language, an irresponsibility of expression as urgent in its way as were the grieving, uncollaborating responsibilities of Beckett's tiny gestures and of Celan's beautifully impacted lines. In all our next books and poems, I am looking forward to the end of lateness, to the end of memory, to an irreverent aphasia in which no word is ever withheld out of guilt or uncertainty. This anticipation is a feeling antithetical to remorse, a feeling very near to love as John Ashbery envisions it in his magnificently profligate prose poem "The New Spirit":

> At this point an event of such glamor and such radiance
> occurred that you forgot the name all over again. It could
> be compared to arriving in an unknown city at night, in-
> toxicated by the strange lighting and the ambiguities of the
> streets. The person sitting next to you turned to you, her
> voice broke and a kind of golden exuberance flooded over
> you just as you were lifting your arm to the luggage rack. At
> once the weight of the other years and above all the weight
> of distinguishing among them slipped away. You found
> yourself not wanting to care. (270)

Having chosen to betray the silence, to deny the murderer's patent upon authority and volume, I find that it is very early now. I find that any word can lead to countless others, none of which is reserved to anyone else's idea of experience. I find that I am in love and that my traitorousness is the fidelity I owe to that love's undetermined, unmuted future. The next poem will tell me how to live in that future, enlarging the time, enlarging the syllables in which it will be voiced, even unto the full status of the entire real. Nothing that is green could venture less, thus early, thus disburdened by betrayal.

Outrageous Innocence/Innocence Outraged

M oderny begins and ends with disappearing children. (A hapless search-party, the postmodern, seeks these little ones all in vain, having no maps but absences and no stars but voided signifiers by which to steer at night.)

Modernity's adventure begins when Huckleberry Finn decides that civilization, for all its cozy doting, is an uninhabitable redundancy, a story only a fool, or criminal, could sit through twice.

> But I reckon I got to light out for the territory ahead of the rest, because Aunt Sally she's going to adopt me and sivilize me, and I can't stand it. I been there before. (Twain 323)

Huck absconds with an innocence intact, as innocence alone has wisdom to know that nothing ever actually happens twice. To remain itself, innocence must remain original, no matter what the cost. And the cost is disappearance, which Huck cheerfully, vigorously accepts. Such cheer and vigor originate our Modernity, meaning a conviction in the now and the never-again and the new. The very last chapter of the novel from which Huck departs into uninscribed adventure is entitled "Nothing more to write," and already I see Arthur Rimbaud smiling, giving up on writing even as he begins, knowing in his soul the only reason for doing a poem is never to do it again: to abandon it, along with all the other poems, to the tender mercies of Aunt Sally; to light out for the unincorporated and unbound territories where poetry is innocent of even every word. So, Modernity begins with an outrageous innocence, a recklessness with nothing but further recklessness in mind, as anything further would be an End.

> *"It began with the laughter of children; it will end there."*
>
> —Rimbaud, *A Season in Hell*, 98

Indeed, yes. At the other end of Modernity is another child and an altogether different sort of disappearance. Inexhaustibly, Nabokov's *Lolita* details the exhaustion of the now, the despoiling of the never-again, the debauching of the new. There's nothing wrong in a grown man's loving little Dolly Haze. [As Rimbaud avows in "Bad Blood"—"the lechery's wonderful." (23)] But there is only catastrophe in his possessing one Lolita. Possession is a redundancy carried out to criminal extremes. Humbert Humbert is not merely a parenthesis with absence at its heart; he is the parodic Adam of an overturned Eden (i.e., the former United States) when he turns to absent Eve for a few last words. In *Paradise Lost*, the original revised Adam says

> How art thou lost, how on a sudden lost,
> Defac't, deflourd, and now to Death devote?
> (Milton IX 900-01)

In *Lolita*, Humbert Humbert, with no innocence, and not even the name of innocence, left to his name, addresses himself to Modernity's still, small demise. His race run, his capture imminent, he leaves his car (no one to witness and adjust) and walks along a hillside, hearing playground voices from the valley below.

> Reader! What I heard was but the melody of children at play, nothing but that . . . I stood listening to that musical vibration from my lofty slope, to those flashes of separate cries with a kind of demure murmur for background, and then I knew that the hopelessly poignant thing was not Lolita's absence from my side, but the absence of her voice from that concord. (Nabokov 308)

So, Modernity ends as an innocence outraged, and Rimbaud says "I told you so." First there is the laughter of children and then there is the laughter from which children, one by one, are made to disappear.

The poet of *A Season in Hell* is both the reckless child at the beginning and the ravished child at the "hopelessly poignant" finish of all things Modern. He was, after all, merely candid and altogether prophetic in his famous imperative: "I must be absolutely modern," that is, Modern from beginning to end. And as is only suitable to the artist playing this dual role, Rimbaud is a figure twice disappeared. He died out of his life as a provincial wunderkind and into that of the *poete maudit*, and then he died again, out of an already famously salacious posterity, into the fierce, mercantile obscurity of real death. His poetry itself absconded twice: once from rigid, artificial conventions mastered early and, so it would seem, effortlessly. ("Jugurtha," a poem in Latin, earned the fourteen-year-old Rimbaud first prize at the *Concours Academique*); and a second time when, although its author was not yet even twenty, the poetry abandoned poems altogether, leaving in its wake debris we rightly honor as the most innovative writing of the past two centuries and more. As with Huck's, as with Lolita's, these disappearances happened on behalf of an innocence outrageous and outraged.

Yet, however angry, however anguished it becomes, the language of *A Season in Hell* never betrays its innocent conviction of Disappearance-as-Sacrament, just as it never strays far or strays long from sacramental language. Nothing prepares a poet half so well for perdition as early Sunday school success. (There is an unforgettable photograph of Arthur seated beside his brother Frederic on the morning of their first communion. Arthur's fist is clenched atop his prayer book, and there is as much terror as there is piety in the child-poet's eyes, as much sorrow as there is smile in the expression on his face.) Rimbaud's book may be a bomb thrown into the quiet purlieus of romance, but if it is indeed a bomb, it is a missal too. We must remember that God's Modernity (i.e., Christianity) also began and ended with a disappearing child. *A Season in Hell* rejoices in the disappearance of the Son of God from Heaven, proclaiming "Christmas on earth!" with unambiguous delight. In this,

Rimbaud keeps faith with the many tender, outraged innocents before him, celebrating the kidnap of divinity by flesh as the surety of godliness in childhood evermore.

> How like an Angel came I down!
>   How bright are all things here!
> When first among his Works I did appear
>   O how their Glory did me crown!
> The world resembled his ETERNITIE,
>   In which my soul did walk;
> And everything that I did see
>   Did with me talk.
>   (Traherne, "Wonder" 1-8)

There is more than a little of Eden in *A Season in Hell*. However damned, every blessed thing in the poem walks and talks. To the pure all things are pure, and it is the furious purity of Rimbaud's gift that enables him to find and to transcribe the ambient wild testaments of which his book is ultimately comprised.

> Not in entire forgetfulness,
> And not in utter nakedness,
> But trailing clouds of glory do we come
> From God, who is our home:
> Heaven lies about us in our infancy!
> (Wordsworth, "Ode: Intimations of Immortality" 62-66)

The stolen child of Heaven brings Heaven with him where he goes, even into Hell. Rimbaud's infancy is the glory of his hell, and no amount of scorching nor the strongest smell of burn entirely conceals the innocent's origin and home—"where every heart flew open and all wines flowed."

CHARLES: God is babyhood.

MR. ALCOTT: There is truth in that, I believe; and yet it is language so liable to be misunderstood, that it had better not be used. (Alcott, *Conversations with Children on the Gospels*, 190)

His innocence intact if under siege, Rimbaud had no need for circumspections. His God is babyhood and has remained so despite a century and more of mordant interpreters and despite the disappearance of poetry (poetry is babyhood too) from his poems. Once it is Christmas, it is always Christmas, or else it is the end of the world. In the meantime, Jack Spicer's simple imperative—"Poet, be like God"—purely echoes Rimbaud's primary sense. Whenever the child who disappeared from Heaven disappears from Earth (or from Hell or from Charleville, Rimbaud's home in the Ardennes—isn't it great that he came from Arden?), it is the End. So, *A Season in Hell* is the end of Rimbaud's writing life. Perhaps Nietzsche was right and Rimbaud knew it: Jesus Christ was the last Christian. Outraged upon a cross, his innocence disappeared into and out of that empty sepulcher long ago. Rimbaud is the latest baby to bring Christmas into Hell where, perhaps, it is Christmas still. But here? Rimbaud isn't telling. He does not speak of second comings. His innocence—like Huck's, like Lolita's, like Christ's—is too absolutely Modern for wishful thinking.

But there is a wish that comes true without our asking, without ever being wished. It takes the form of a law best loved by the lawless (imagine here a lengthy discourse on the history of antinomianism) and by the bringers of good news (insert Christ's words to the woman taken in adultery or, if you prefer, chapter 7 of *The Wind in the Willows*: "The Piper at the Gates of Dawn"). Call it "The Law of Conservation of Innocence," a law that rhymes with the mysteries of energy and matter, plainly stating that innocence can neither be created nor destroyed. So, when innocence has gone it has not gone away but, rather, gone on. In this sense, disappearance means only an increase in velocity, and so Rimbaud may both honor his imperative—"I must be absolutely Modern" (*A Season in Hell* 79)—and be an outraged disappearing innocent still. (No contradiction either, then, in juxtaposing "It is finished" with the more comfortable "I am with you always.") Upholding this Law of Conservation of Innocence as doggedly and beautifully as it does, *A Season in Hell*, for me, is Modernity's best and most unequivocal furthering of the bold projects of William Blake. In fact, it is Rimbaud's deep and widely unacknowledged affinities with the poet of "The Tyger" and "The Lamb" and "The Divine Image" that made me keen to attempt a translation and this essay afterwards. I guess you could say that everything I know about innocence I began to know in Blake; it was Blake who taught me how to love the Gospels, and it was Blake again who helped me to take Kerouac at his word and know that "Beat" is surely and forever shorthand for "Beatific." Blake is the portal open in every direction and the wide, high way. Huck is there on a hayride with Lolita, etc., etc. W.H. Stevenson, in his warm, good introduction to the Penguin edition of Blake's selected poetry puts the case well:

> . . . from Thel to America Blake presents his case: the indestructibility of innocence. The soul that freely follows imaginative instincts will be innocent and virtuous; nature protects this innocence, and the only sin is to allow one's nature to be perverted by law and custom. (14)

The poet of *A Season in Hell* is a nature poet, once we accept Nature as the protector of all innocents. The poet of *A Season in Hell* is a moralist, once we know morality survives by the transcendence of law, and triumphs in the overthrow of custom. The poet of *A Season in Hell* is Blakean to his bones, once we feel his energy as imaginative instinct unbound by any virtue save the free force driving. A chariot of fire is a goddamn big car every time.

Goofy as it sounds, whenever I picture Rimbaud, I see the brother in one soul and one body to William Blake's Oothoon, the outraged heroine of *Visions of the Daughters of Albion* (1793). Raped by Bromion, Oothoon nevertheless wisely and wildly maintains the fact of her innocence with all virgin purity intact. To her despairing beloved, Theotormon, she avows:

> ". . . Arise my Theotormon; I am pure,
> Because the night is gone that closed me in its deadly black.
> ....
> How can I be defiled when I reflect your image pure?
> Sweetest the fruit the worm feeds on, and the soul preyed on by woe,
> The new-washed lamb tinged with the village smoke, and the

bright swan
By the red earth of our immortal river. I bathe my wings,
And I am white and pure to hover round Theotormon's
breast."

(II. 59-60; 85–89)

A Season in Hell proposes a strange but unperplexed journey into purity through deadly black. It savors the sweetness in the
mouths of worms. It catches the smell of burn upon new-washed
lambs. Always its purposes are flight and flight and flight with velocities ever increasing and unseen wings ever more strong and
white. The ultimate victory announced in the closing figures of
"Farewell" declares Rimbaud's unquestionable kinship with the
Oothoon who cries aloud—

> Does not the worm erect a pillar in the moldering
>   churchyard,
> And a palace of eternity in the jaws of the hungry grave?
> Over his porch these words are written: "Take thy bliss,
>   O Man!
> And sweet shall be thy taste; and sweet thy infant joys renew!"
> Infancy, fearless, lustful, happy! nestling for delight
> In laps of pleasure. Innocence! honest, open, seeking
> The vigorous joys of morning light, open to virgin bliss.

(II. 160–66)

Rimbaud's freedom is the improved infancy Oothoon
believes. Rimbaud's truth, the restored integrity of his body and
his soul is the unassailable virginity she proves. Our angel-headed
hipster of the Ardennes and Aden was surely lovingly foreshadowed in Hercules Buildings, Lambeth, circa 1793. William was
Arthur's friend in Albion.

And Arthur finds a later friend, quite near to us in space
and time, though half a world away from Charleville. Living and
working in Big Sur, Henry Miller composed what is likely to remain the most tender and most exact appreciation of Rimbaud in
the English language. In *The Time of the Assassins* (whose title comes
from the final line of "Morning of Drunkenness," the self-same
poem in which the author of *Illuminations* avows—"It began with the

laughter of children; it will end there"), Miller summons his subject into the embrace of a further poetry disguised as prose disguised as criticism. Such sympathy and understanding rise to the level of ecstasy, and I can only urge you to read what I cannot hope and have no wish to paraphrase. There are, however, two very short passages I must not fail to share, if only in the spirit of full disclosure and simple tact. I see Rimbaud by the light of these passages, and I feel the fact of him flourishing in the mysteries Henry Miller shows. The first is this: "He is the father of many schools and the parent of none.(p. 58) These words disclose the secret of Rimbaud's new and further virginity as the poet/soul of undisclosed, innumerable futures. The pure poet inspires endlessly even as he remains entirely, almost apocalyptically innocent of posterity. His issues are not issues of control. His concerns are unconcerned with aftermath. So, he is nothing more or less than purely candid when he declares that "action is not life but, rather, a waste of energy." Always exemplary, never instructive, *A Season in Hell* remains a vision rather than a tool, one always too glad to embarrass the head or heart committed to its use: "There's nothing to be done. / I belong to happiness, body and soul." ("O Seasons, O Chateaux" 9-10) Looking upon the poets who've come after him, Rimbaud seems to say, like a very wry archangel, "They don't look like me." How could they? There is no sharing, no passing down a happiness whose first premise is to disappear.

Here is the second passage from *The Time of the Assassins* whose light I must somehow reflect:

> He is the only writer whom I have read and reread with undiminished joy and excitement, always discovering something new in him, always profoundly touched by his purity. (Miller, 108)

Here, the word "only" resounds with its original meaning, that is, "one-ly," as in the virginal integrity inside of which *A Season in Hell* disappears. Here, "joy and excitement" efface and supersede understanding as does the laughter of children, as do the notes of that "fabulous opera" Rimbaud intends no ears to hear. Finally, it is here that Miller establishes "purity" as that means of contact by which poetry sets innocence into eternal motion, which is itself unmoved by any motive, by undiminished joy, by undiminished excitement. There is no friction and no fiction. Miller's love for Arthur Rimbaud is far too good to be anything but true.

I must admit I had a wonderful time translating this poem, and a wonderful time too in fabulating the contexts and correspondences of my pleasure. As John Ashbery has written, "We are fabulous beasts after all," meaning, I believe, that poets and the readers of poetry (who must be poets too) are animals inclined to self-astonishment and to the giddy broadcast of that astonishment amongst their fellow beasts. How else could it be that poetry breaks free of language, becoming the onomatopoeia of the soul? How else could poems sometimes so utterly revise our notion of humanness that we emerge from them as blissful strangers to ourselves? But now it's time to turn this essay over to its sole owner and proprietor, Arthur Rimbaud. I have not imagined his innocence, nor have I fabulated his perfect fidelity to the ideals and practices of purity. He is the child who disappeared because he said so and lived (and died) to tell the tale. He is the accelerator of child-likeness because his writing attained such speeds, inscribed such wild and redemptive velocities. Time now to honor his speed in a montage (with quickest commentary) of passages from his poem. I cannot give him the last word, because this is English. But all the better words, and each and every lustrous trajectory, originate with him.

> Once last innocence . . . one last diffidence. It's done. Please don't publish my disgust and my treasons.
>
> (Rimbaud 27)

A Season in Hell almost literally begins at an ending and a disappearing point. "It's done" makes a chilling rhyme with Jesus' "It is finished." And that's the energy source, the agent of acceleration. Rimbaud's crucifixion predates his poem, is external to it. (This is why he's always outraged but never angry, always in full cry but never shrill.) His purposes in Hell are its harrowing. Of what? Disgusts and treasons. By what? Apocalyptic innocence made to last. The very last thing Rimbaud would wish of posterity is the hysterical institutionalization of his lousy life. For him, poetry is the afterlife of innocence, that is, its Real Life, with all the hallucinations of Hell dispelled and nothing but Heavens after Heaven in full view.

> Shall I not be carried off like a baby into the paradise of
> oblivion and play?
>
> (Rimbaud 31)

The afterlife of innocence is poetry dearly oblivious to all the horrors of the Hells it harrowed. There's no more work to do. Small wonder then that *A Season in Hell* is the last poem Rimbaud ever writes. Small wonder that it already shines with the luster of a child gone out to play, of a boy playing hooky from the tedium (and *Te Deum*) of literary culture. When you read his poem closely and with an eye to fun, a mind to mischief, it capers and cartwheels. Its paradise is a playground, not an empyrean. How else account for similes such as these?

> . . . like a mirror when the lamp next door begins to move, like
> treasure in the forest!
>
> (Rimbaud 29)

Parsing such figures, the reader becomes a figure of fun. What does a mirror make of the lamp next door? Where are we to look to find its light? Into the unreflecting mirror? Into the further room towards which it cannot move? Indeed, I know the simile could be made to work and so become the distracted ghost of a reflection. But Rimbaud makes no pause for any acumen or labor. No, he hurries us outside into the forest for a treasure hunt. If we go willingly, we are cheerfully bewildernessed. Something wonderful happens to treasure when it's in a forest, though I couldn't for the life of me tell you what. There's something Edenic about forests with treasures in them, though anybody's guess about Eden is as good as mine. Rimbaud's Hell is conjured by poetry that unconjures it more quickly than we can know. In the paradise of oblivion and play, artistry is not burdened by craftsmanship. Metaphor and simile do not accumulate, do not struggle towards an argument or sum. Instead, they simply accelerate the pleasures of the game. (What, do you think, would Huckleberry Finn have made of all the purgative legwork in Dante's *Commedia*? Meeting the venerable Roman poet in a dark wood late one evening, what wisecrack would Lolita crack to Vergil?) Innocence hotfoots Hell with only fun at heart. The poetry gets carried away with itself and, in Hell, that's a very good outcome for a game.

Soberly now, let us appraise the true extent of my innocence.
(Rimbaud 33)

I have never seen anything more serious or sober than a child with a toy. Have a look sometime at a little picture by Hieronymus Bosch called *Child with Whirligig*—it might as well be a photograph of Arthur Rimbaud's soul. Nothing's as strategically exacting or tactically exhausting as playing hooky. (Do you remember?) Innocence is reckless, not stupefied. Unintoxicated, a pure soul moves towards oblivion like the god it surely is.

Rimbaud has his purposes in *A Season in Hell*, and these purposes are neither clandestine nor obscure. The bourgeois espionage of "art that conceals art" has no appeal to a poet whose disappearing act is true. Rimbaud proposes an Innocence Militant, a manifest destiny of the pure of heart. Therefore, everything's riding on "true extent." How far into eternity can innocence shine a light? According to *A Season in Hell*, nothing short of all the way. How much reality is the just and proper portion of the pure? According to *A Season in Hell*, nothing less than all of it. The poem is tireless. (Nowhere have I ever encountered such and so many exclamations; one of my greatest challenges in translating was to overcome a deeply inculcated shyness of exclamation points.) The poem is voracious. (One of my greatest pleasures has been the imagistic gluttony Rimbaud approves.) The poem is a fanatic (from the Latin *fanaticus*, i.e. pertaining to a temple) in the cause of all things happy and harmless. Our age has lost the gift of zeal, having too often accepted ideological talking points in bad exchange. The zealous program of *A Season in Hell* is the unprogrammatic imperium of the newborn—"newborn' being, *sans aucun doute*, a synonym for "absolutely modern." In the third chapter of the Gospel of Saint John, Jesus says to Nicodemus, "Except a man be born again, he cannot see the kingdom of God." What else do you call a man who has been born again but "newborn?" To Nicodemus, Jesus counseled an absolute modernity, an innocence extended without end. Carried off like a baby, Rimbaud advances with an equal zeal.

> My innocence is enough to make me weep.
> (Rimbaud 35)

The purity of *A Season in Hell* is such that it commands a fine and physical distinction between pathos and poignancy. Rimbaud wades, but he never wallows. Weeping for his innocence, he expounds neither self-pity nor remorse. Rather, he objectifies the circumstance of innocence in this world: not a matter for sympathy (pathos), but a matter of simple pain (poignancy). The career of innocence (ask Huckleberry, ask Lolita) is agonized without anguish. There is no leisure for egotistical sublimes. Birth is busy. The newborn finds a way, and outrage is an altogether different discourse from complaint. The case is put clearly in Rimbaud's famous dictum of 13 May 1871:

> Je est un autre. Tant pis pour le bois qui se trouve violon . . . .
> I is one other. Too bad for the wood that finds itself a violin . . .
> (Rimbaud, *Letters* 28)

Rimbaud weeps for his innocence, but the innocence he weeps for is not Rimbaud's. It belongs to another whose continuous rebirth follows a separate trajectory from the rebirths of an Arthur whose poems were scarcely a moment, an incidental adventure below the words. This is the grandeur and almost unaccountable lightsomeness of *A Season in Hell*—pain purged of persona; torment abolished by its first and, sequentially, by its every outcry. Such purity might be terrifying. (Indeed, I think it does terrify some readers, including some of Rimbaud's most fervent admirers—so much so that they demonize him to domesticate him; after all, a sadist is easier to live with than an angel, though almost no one could survive the saying so.) Such purity is, however, in the companionship of its velocity and the cordiality of its imaged faith, not terror but tenderness—an innocent weeping for joy at the triumph of all the innocence in this world. "Let us welcome, then, an influx of new strength and real tenderness. Come the dawn, armed with our ardent patience, we enter magnificent cities."

At the velocities of faith and tenderness, purity is no mere state of being. It becomes behavior, an accelerated waking to more light and purer light. In this sense, vision, even the simplest opening of an eye, motives a cleansing and rebirth. It's what Thoreau referred to in the opening of *Walden*'s "The Pond in Winter," declaring "I awoke to an answered question, to Nature and daylight." Nearer to our own time, it shines in Robert Creeley's famous anecdote about waking up one morning upon a patch of grass beside the Pacific Ocean after a night's dissipation, there to find Jack Kerouac (Rimbaud's most nearly perfect and devoted American ephebe) beaming down, inquiring "Are you pure?" At the speed of poetry, purity is up to something. And what that something really is and actually accomplishes affirms the happiness of *A Season in Hell*.

> At last, O happiness, O reason, I expelled the azure, which is a darkness, from the sky, and then I lived, a spark of gold of purest light.
>
> (Rimbaud, *A Season in Hell* 61)

To see the light is to become the light, when seeing outspeeds the darkness of metaphor and finds the sun and the sky. Rimbaud is self-alchemized by his pure eyes. He resists the arch-symbolists' temptation of "azure"—just try to get through even a page of French poetry of the nineteenth-century without confronting that impossible and tired jeweler's blue—and in resisting becomes a force for the liberation of purity and the transformation of life into light. Literally, then, Rimbaud proves to be a poet of The Enlightenment, one for whom the virtues of Happiness and Reason are not, however, the periwigged and wishful thinking of constitutional conventions but, instead, vivid first principles of human innocence waking and remaining awake. Again, it is impossible not to think of William Blake—the Blake who railed against timid enlightenments such as those Voltaire allowed. Candide's innocence was an irony. Oothoon's was iron-clad. Voltaire hoed a patch of garden. Blake painted Edens in pure gold. Rimbaud, in *A Season in Hell*, goes Blake one better: not only in becoming gold himself, but by alchemizing his goldenness—with only the outrageous conviction of his perfect innocence for an alembic—into a purity true enough to extinguish the old virtues and to spark fires in the new.

> O purity! purity!
> It is these moments of awakening that give me visions of purity!
> (*A Season in Hell* 71)

Rimbaud's alchemy is a supernatural sobriety, the eye of a newborn opening upon a nature no one's seen before. The unprecedented expels all metaphors, all azures. Its poetry needs no further poems. As Charles Olson, himself a fine if circumstantial translator of Rimbaud, avows in "La Preface:" "We are the newborn, and there are no flowers."

A *Season in Hell* is the first and final testament, then, of a sovereign baby. No surprise at all that, among its stridently innumerable exclamations, one should resound most volubly and most long:

> Christmas on earth!
> (*A Season in Hell* 75)

Christmas is the feast-day of the newly opened eye. It is the festival of first lights in the deepest darkness. It is a synonym for innocence and also for every peril innocence must outface. It celebrates the possibly infinite expanse of one very particular morning, even to the end of time. So, in a very real sense, it marks the End of Time—a quiet apocalypse summoned out of heaven by a newborn's cry. It is the abolition of winter and of seasons in themselves. It is the abolition of adulthood, at least so far as heaven is concerned. It is also the abolition of humanity as an enterprise, a substitution of angelic nature for the tired copulations of mortal women and men. John Milton knew it. In "On the Morning of Christ's Nativity," he details, with truly disturbing enthusiasm and youthful vigor, the systematic devastation of antiquity and all its ideals and its movements and its gods by a single drowsy baby and his squadron of "Bright-harnest Angels." Milton's Jesus is an *enfant terrible*, surely and with a vengeance—the redoubtable precursor of our young poet of *A Season in Hell*. Christmas, as proclaimed by Arthur Rimbaud, unlooses innocence from the bondage of nations and nature, of genders and engendering. Balzac knew it. In *Seraphita* (surely the only great French novel set in a Norwegian fjord), he conjures a hermaphroditic angel to confound the truisms and bywords of romantic literary culture. Utterly self-contained, Seraphita is "both innocent and learned," a protagonist having nothing to do with agony, a character beyond character and law. It's a great pleasure to note that, among the many ways by which Seraphita mystifies his/her Lutheran compatriots, signal is a strange reluctance to attend church services on any day but Christmas Day. Celebrating "Christmas on earth" at the climax of *A Season in Hell*, Rimbaud rejoices in the utterly transformed prospects of Innocence in the apocalyptic and catastrophizing circumstance of Absolute Modernity. On Christmas morning, Innocence wakes to find itself Divine and to know itself as a gender of one entirely, "free to possess the truth in one soul and one body." (Rimbaud, *A Season in Hell* 79) The disappearing child is a child forever now: a god and a new nature, safe and secure from all alarm. Poetry is a child forever too, no longer supervised or circumscribed by the measures of any verse. Christmas, at least as far as our Arthur is concerned, means the abolition of poems too. In the Edenic and imperishable circumstance of Absolute Poetry (Rimbaud is the laureate of Absolutes—relativists have no business and no access here), the metaphors are idle and a poem is the devil's workshop.

Am I wrong?

(A Season in Hell 77)

To write or to translate or, if I've read rightly, even to read Rimbaud's *A Season in Hell*, is—to paraphrase a beautiful passage of Lawrence Ferlinghetti's—constantly to risk absurdity. Children are wise in their despotism, keeping a constant watchfulness over the playfulness of their play. An angel can never be too careful of its carelessness. Once Lucifer conceived a purpose, he was lost. And there is no greater risk in this or any world than innocence, refusing, as it does, ever to use the satanic tools experience places so teasingly, so craftily to hand. And what, please tell me if you know, could be more absurd than to prize, above any other poetry, a poetry that revokes all future poems? I am almost afraid to take Rimbaud at his word; although, so far as I can tell, he refuses to be taken any other way. If I look for outlets or for irony, *A Season in Hell* will strike me dead with shame. In the very last figure of his very great poem, Rimbaud claims a "great advantage" I've found impossible to deny him: he can laugh. The advantages of every advantage known to humankind collapse under the sound. In the peaceable kingdom of the eternally disappearing child, laughter opens hearts, and love flows out.

Canon Fodder

Ibelieve in the poignancy of reading, a thing I first imagined when I saw the closing moments of François Truffaut's *Fahrenheit 451*. Tenderly, lyrically, the camera follows men and women walking in a snowy woodland as all recite, in a future where books must burn, the books they have become. My teaching has taken much instruction from the image. I urge my student poets each to become a canon unto himself or herself. Surely, an education in poetry, a life in poetry, is simply this: the unique assembly or concord of poems present whenever a poem is read or whenever one is newly written. The nine poems I've chosen here are strong in my assembly and essential to the concord I prize. They are, variously, poems of landscape, and in the passages of landscape, they severally happen upon true Faith and upon the reality of Happiness. Nine pastorals, then, and not a shepherd to be seen.

1. "The Yellowhammer's Nest" by John Clare

Much is made of the pathos of John Clare's madness and of the quiet courage with which he endured it. His much-anthologized poem "I Am" embodies these magnificently. But we could never attend enough to the greater body of his works: poems characterized by the serenity of a steady, loving gaze. Among these is a wonderful sequence devoted to birds' nests. To my mind, "The Yellowhammer's Nest" is the masterpiece. Here, close attention to minute detail—"Five eggs pen-scribbled over lilac shells"—leads to a discovery of identity when Clare embraces the yellowhammer as a fellow poet. And from identity flows compassion, and with compassion comes the peace and sanity of perfect understanding.

2. "The Mango Tree" by Hart Crane

The final years of Hart Crane's writing life have largely been abducted by biography and biographical speculation. The promise and autodidactic innovations of *White Buildings* are much praised, even as the vaunting, catastrophic ambitions of *The Bridge* are well beloved. But among the later poems, only "The Broken Tower" has entered the canon. At the end of his life, Crane was writing no mere coda. There is a playfulness, a colloquial intimacy and ease in so many of his last poems that it is impossible not to find in them a lucent forecast of the Beats and the New York School and all the best mischief of postmodernism. "Up jug to musical, hanging jug just gay spiders" anticipates so much, even as it delights in the moment of its sound. And there are many such moments in "The Mango Tree."

3. "My Father Photographed with Friends" by William Bronk

In the poetry of William Bronk, meanings stride forward through particulars, forever warm with the striving. His is the plainsong of an undeceived, deep faith in details. In this poem Bronk assembles God and man, mortality, and all the wishful thinking behind the camera until the poem inclines toward an eternity it cannot prove or show. The poignancy of reading knows its keenest pathos here. "God sweeten the bitter judgments of our lives. We wish so much."

4. "An Altogether Different Language" by Anne Porter

When I first added the poems of Anne Porter to the syllabus of my New York Poets seminars, the students were flummoxed and a bit cross. How could such transparency and unadornment jibe with the extravagant indirections so vividly deployed by Ashbery, O'Hara, and Koch? But then . . . but then . . .

The same calm, levitated isolations and the "gestural realism" that we so value in the paintings of her husband, Fairfield Porter, drift through this poem like little portions of miracle. Her lines are each a place apart, but mutually aware and awaiting concord, something "we have still to learn."

5. "The Bluet" by James Schuyler

And if we speak of portions of miracle, we must speak very soon of James Schuyler. I can say it without reservation: "The Bluet" is a perfect poem. Here the quiet timeliness of eternity breaks forth as a particular flower and then, by miracle, becomes a friend. Poetic authority is simply the stamina of attention surcharged by color, circumstance, and sense. The upshot is shattering: "That bluet breaks / me up."

6. "Harp Trees" by Robin Blaser

Beginning in the 1950s and continuing to the present day, Robin Blaser has been assembling an epic of increments, wholly unaggressive: *The Holy Forest*. It is an epic of purely lyrical events whose heroic virtue adventures amity among all figures in a lyric's field. In "The Harp Trees," amity finds "a kind of speech / at the edge of thought," and with that speech it moves outward in many directions (including memory, including metamorphosis), encountering everywhere and in every thing "kindness" and "greenness." I have never, in any other poem, experienced such a gentle transformation. And yet the transformation is absolute.

7. "Letter from the Mountains" by James K. Baxter

This is the closing piece from the New Zealand poet's final collection, *Runes*, composed at Jerusalem, a Maori settlement to which Baxter had been summoned in a dream and from which, having abandoned his university position, he went out as a social worker to the drug-addicted and the poor. Here, amity begins as the forgotten message of amity and becomes a pilgrim. Like Bunyan's Pilgrim, Baxter abandons his City of Destruction and makes his way to "[t]he mountain that has taken [his] being to itself." This is allegory without symbolizing: real thorns and rocks and tears. And so the allegory is endlessly immediate, always open: "My door has forgotten how to shut."

8. "What the Leaf Told Me" by Ronald Johnson

Ronald Johnson was the William Blake of erasure, palimpsest, and collage, an American Visionary Museum unto himself. Beginning with a passage from *The Diary of the Reverend Francis Kilvert* (an all-too-little-known masterwork of the 19th century), this poem unfolds a moment of effortless amazement into telling brightness. Bedazzlement begins to rival the sun. And then the brightness comes to rest "In a Wren's Eye." This is a poem that Plotinus (who once said, "Nothing not exactly like the sun can see the sun") would have rejoiced to read.

9. "O Heart Uncovered" by Joseph Ceravolo

The deep delight of Ceravolo's poetry is all in distances instantaneously traversed. This poem moves from "snow range" to an "Arizona room," from wintry bedazzlement to desert darkness, in something short of the blink of an eye. And the movement, like a heartbeat, outspeeds knowledge. "O Heart Uncovered" wears itself on an unraveling sleeve. And the unraveling is Vision. When it ends, "we see the mountains."

Toys and Planets: Joseph Cornell and the Contemporary Poet

Whenever a lyric poem rises above the confines of its emotional occasion or chosen form, it is because of some extraordinary quality of attention—sometimes willed, sometimes wonderfully accidental—on the part of the poet. It is through attention that the lyric makes a virtue of its limits, discovers in a relatively small and admittedly private collection of things and sensations something more than a personal truth. The point of seeing, as Eliot sees that roses have "the look of flowers that are looked at" ("Burnt Norton" 27) or as Ashbery sees that the soul of a portrait "fits/Its hollow perfectly: its room, our moment of attention" ("Self-Portrait in a Convex Mirror" 45-46), is not merely to emphasize some unique acuteness of insight nor to exalt transience to the level of vatic experience. "Burnt Norton" and "Self-Portrait in a Convex Mirror," extensive as they are, depend not upon range but upon attention to a few figures—the rose garden, Parmigianino's painting—for the lyric authority they exercise over our poetry. Authority in the lyric is the result of attention. It cannot claim the epic's sense of cultural consensus nor the drama's sense of a shared experience in time. It depends wholly upon the effect of what and how it sees. Eliot can risk the moral and historical assertions of "Burnt Norton" only because he has discovered a vivid and objective phenomenology *inside* a lyric place and moment, inside the afternoon in the garden. Ashbery can propound the uncomfortably accurate aesthetic and psychological ideals of his poem because he first discovers a similarly vivid phenomenology in the distortions of space and time between himself and the mannerist self-portrait.

The ability to draw something like a philosophy from what is seen and what, once seen, is paid a passionate attention, characterizes the most successfully ambitious lyric poems of our time. Yet more and more, the lyric becomes a province of diminished expectations. Terms such as "assertion" and "authority" only discomfit or outrage the modest, sincere witness the contemporary lyric usually models. And a modesty of witness, consciously or not, implies a modesty of attention. That is why so many poets find themselves drawn to the visual arts—to experience there the authority of works that simply cannot afford to practice or to permit any modesty of attention. There is one modern artist, Joseph Cornell, who seems to me singularly representative of methods of attention so powerfully sympathetic to the methods of lyric that he exercises a hugely beneficial influence and enchantment over poets anxious to uphold the authority of their art.

> The tiny is the last resort of the tremendous.
>
> —Richard Howard, "Closet Drama: An Aporia for Joseph Cornell," 17

I first experienced Cornell's work as a splendid resort from one of the coldest January days in New York history. Stepping into the Museum of Modern Art's 1980–1981 Cornell exhibition from the vertical, frozen, and annihilating sunlight of Fifty-Third Street, I found myself in a comforting tropic of miniatures, of small warm places made to shelter the lives of objects and of human names. This is the primary quality of Cornell's attention: affection, an understanding that the business of art is rescue. Cornell does not just rescue toys and discards of the world from the drift of contextlessness; he rescues worlds themselves by reuniting cosmos and object, the human image with the homemade particulars that evidence and support the authority of the human. In each of his works, the motive for such rescue is love as St. Augustine understood it: the desire simply that a thing exist. To exist, things must have a place and a sustaining network of relations. Those are just what the boxes of Joseph Cornell provide. Within his constructions, the tiny lends its particular being to the tremendous; the idea of cosmos is rescued through its relations to toys. In his "Soap Bubble Sets" of the 1940s, elegant, useless toy pipes, marbles, and seashells frame antique maps of the moon, the solar system, and the stars. Abstract universals are thus domesticated, made part of the human world in acquiring the familiar status of objects. Thus, familiar objects also reclaim their rightful share of the infinite and mysterious, escaping the contexts of child's play to float among planets and suns.

This rearrangement of contexts, this liberation of the familiar within the exotic and the exotic within the familiar is an essential of lyric. It is where lyric really begins, loosing sensation into the world and admitting the immediate world into the tiny cosmos of sensibility. The lyric begins to pay attention by practicing the original unspoken premise of Cornell's constructions, by looking outside of pre-existing contexts for the self, for what is real, and for that new place—the poem—where they can join.

> . . . So too the body is a box
> which holds the heart and is
> crowded with absence.
>   (Susan Wood, "For Joseph Cornell" 9-12)

The lyric does not accomplish its re-vision of the real simply by crowding its stanzas with liberated objects and freshly indeterminate versions of the self. A further quality of attention and of authority arises from a poem's acknowledgement that it is itself a context, a limiting spatial metaphor no matter how porous its structure to time and subjectivity. Many contemporary poets abrogate attention and abdicate authority in denying the spatial metaphor shapes of words must finally be. They do so from honorable intentions, wishing not to misrepresent either thought or sensation, both of which are transients in language, "momentary in the mind." But inevitable form need not be denied to preserve the integrity of context. Cornell's boxes never apologize for their spatiality. They are rooms, fixed stanzas willed into the forms in which we find them. Among the freed toys, stars, and portraits, there is room for contingency and transience. Cornell accommodates them as absences, just as the human heart accommodates them.

The objects present in the boxes receive their new contexts and new authority partly from the pressure of the absence crowded around them like an atmosphere, the pressure of what is not there—what change, accident, and will have deprived them of or liberated them from—redoubling the pressure of what so astonishingly *is* there. Transience as the pressure of absence is most beautifully reified in Cornell's hotel boxes: "Hotel de l'Etoile," "Hotel du Cygne," and others. These constructions seem to be furnished by anticipation of occupancy. They are empty except for their tantalizing names and a minimal décor, open to whatever transient significance the passing viewer may select to fill them. Cornell offers a further lesson to the lyric in these. The poet does not necessarily have to assume the full burden of thought's transience and sensation's brevity. The fact of interpretation guarantees him reliable partners in their support, as all spatial metaphor is ever adrift in interpretation. Let the poet pay attention to those atmospheres of absence crowded around his subjects and words. They too are himself and what is real in the new poem, the lyrical hotel.

> You are always a little too
> young to understand. He is
> bored with his sense of the
> past, the artist. Out of the
> prescient rock in his heart
> he has spread a land without
> flowers of near distances.
>
> (Frank O'Hara, "Joseph Cornell" 8-14)

All that is needed to complete a poem's atmosphere and a poet's phenomenology is a version of time. Too often, having managed a difficult, almost heroic attention, poems falter in the end by electing a version of time that inhibits the *exercise* of authority. Some, like Wordsworth, suspend their poems in pastness. Their poems shrink into retrospectives. Some, like the Imagists, detail an absolute present and make a poetry of vignettes and cameos. As Richard Howard has written (in the poem cited above), "writing happens to happen in time." Emphasis is on the verb "happens," the sense of time as an enactment originating in the past, continuing through the present toward the future. This version of time, time as a medium of enactment, acknowledges the full history of subject and object, what they are as well as what they were (through absence), and what they might become within the poem.

This may be Cornell's final lesson to the poet: that having rescued himself and the things of his world, having devotedly animated his sense of the past, he should not forget to turn and face the daunting emptiness of futurity ("a land without / flowers of near distances" [13-14]) where change, which is already real, already present in his stanza's little room, may alter him and his objects beyond all recognition. It is a lesson taught by a tremendously moving series of later works called "Window Facades," each of which is a barred box looking into nothing. The boxes are not empty; they contain perspective, pastness and present, in containing their glass and latticework arranged as windows. But they also contain an emptiness which, because it is unattached to any toy or planet or face, can only be the future. In these constructions, Cornell uses material to remember the future of material. That is what poets must finally do with language. They must learn to use its significations (presence) and silences (absence) not merely to rescue the past and to respect the present, but to remember the future, the emptiness where poem and interpretation disappear into one another, tenderly.

Their Smiles Intact: A Canon's Afterlife

Le Paradis n'est pas artificiel
States of mind are inexplicable to us.
(The Pisan Cantos LXXVI 242–43)

I find myself not wanting to explain, but still to articulate. My present state is a quietness lacking neither voices nor music, though often wordless. Or I could say I'm standing still to listen within a single protracted word, within a pause to be articulated as the land to which I go. This word appears where canon ends. Instead of explanations, then, questions arise. What sort of poetry, what sort of poet, continues here? To be themselves, poems must own ground: their local habitation and proper names. Always, to my mind, flowers are the borders of that ground and therefore of the questions. Flowers blazon images, first emblems of affirmation. Shelley, in Pisa (*"le Paradis n'est pas artificiel"*) and on the borders of a quietness all his own, gave his mind over to one Matilda gathering flowers and the instance of her nearly wordless flower-song: Dante's *Purgatorio*, Canto XX-VIII. I likewise, almost originally, find myself precisely, fixedly there. I cannot read it enough. The canto on the brink of Paradise, a pause without dimensions whose only explanation is itself: a word foreshadowed by a garden.

Only the imparadised can comprehend intensity and continuity as leisure. Yet, at the beginning of *Purgatorio* XX-VIII, in sight of Eden, Dante stands near enough to Paradise to glimpse as much. He explores the new motion, finding it the perfect embodiment of dense and greeny stillness. In Allen Mandelbaum's peerless contemporary English—

Now keen to search within, to search around
 that forest—dense, alive with green, divine—
which tempered the new day before my eyes,
 without delay, I left behind the rise
and took the plain, advancing slowly, slowly
across the ground where every part was fragrant.

Finding myself not wanting to explain, but still to articulate, I am searching for the slower words and the densest lines, not to be difficult, but to be engrossed within a state that is the edge of finale. I want to speak to the intensity of almost nothing left to say. After such a long and difficult arising, Dante finds a level plain. It is dense and alive, in every part fragrant. Its continuity requires no effort at all, even as the poet's senses brook no delay. Dante is at the end of himself, to the extent that his self has been a canon, piloted by Virgil, later joined by Statius, moving. In Pisa, near the end of himself, Shelley chose to translate these same lines as simulacra of his own flamboyant edge.

And earnest to explore within—around—
The divine wood, whose thick green living woof
Tempered the young day to the sight—I wound

Up the green slope, beneath the forest's roof,
With slow, soft steps leaving the mountain's steep,
And sought those inmost labyrinths, motion-proof

Against the air, that in that stillness deep
And solemn, struck upon my forehead bare,
The slow, soft stroke of a continuous . . .
    ("Matilda Gathering Flowers, II. 1–9)

The word "around," coupled with "within," profuses a density soon confirmed by "inmost labyrinths." And twice Shelley, like Dante ("lento, lento") emphasizes the slowness with which poetry now approaches and savors this finale. (Justly, inevitably it would seem, Shelley's very last verses—the fragments of "The Triumph of Life"—would be written in Dante's measure and according to a Dantesque scenario.) Canon closes in. In Canto XXVIII, although he does not know it, Dante has taken a step beyond the limits of Statius and Virgil. Although he does not know it, they have nothing more to say. Richard Holmes, Shelley's finest biographer, describes his subject's crisis days in Pisa as showing "Shelley's need to draw support and stimulation from more purely literary sources" (*Shelley: The Pursuit*, 612). Hence his decision to begin translating Dante, and his most *telling* decision to begin with *Purgatorio* XXVIII: the brink of an ending. Support, needfully, withdraws in the moment of most need. At its limits, canon becomes most dense, most intense. Words slow. Lines profuse inwards. There are nearly too many flowers to be named.

I cannot explain my state of mind, but my peculiar canon—a lifetime's reading, a life *as* reading—leans towards me lovingly, and on a breath of something paradisal (poems, flowers) it whispers articulation. I think of Shelley in the last years of his writing life because he was the poet who figured most forcefully at the beginning of my own. His Ariel image was possibility, and his line was a perfect animal leaping. In graduate school, I owned two copies of the Holmes biography, so as never to be far. The fact that, in his last years, Shelley turned to Dante as I have lately turned with an almost exclusive passion, helps me and schools me, shedding Light whose explanation, as always, is itself. That Shelley should have turned specifically to *Purgatorio* XXVIII, translating the fragment that Mary Shelley later named "Matilda Gathering Flowers," heartens me more than I can say. But Shelley tried to say, and Dante *did*. Here is where my canon leans very close. Coming to the end of poetry as he has loved and understood it, Dante, on the margin of Eden, sees across waters a woman gathering flowers. She sings a song whose words are purely sounds to him—lovely sounds. It is a pivot moment, and a vast, slow pause: hence the leisure of "around" and "within" and the "inmost labyrinths, motion proof." I feel my state of mind as a lavish enigma prior to departure, a conclusion prior to an end. The poetry I want is an afterword to the poems I have made. Matilda's flowers and her wordless, enchanting vocables put the case perfectly. In *Purgatorio* XXVIII, forecast from my beginnings by Shelley's end,

Dante articulates the state of canons advancing upon farewell "across the ground where every part was fragrant."

These intensities of fragrance and of music, in their deep affiliation to the ends of canon, are foregrounded before Dante ever hears Matilda sing. Throughout the *Commedia*, poetry is a filial matter, an autobiographical vow expressed as cosmos. In his epic's quest for a continuing city, Virgil fathered his Florentine successor; now he guides him towards the *Civitas Dei* a pagan cannot know but may sometimes approach as the shadowy backward of Christian ravishment. Continuity is leisure, yes, but there is an eternity of difference between Virgil's leisure among the virtuous pagans and the dense engrossment of his pilgrim ephebe in Paradise. One is resignation; the other is bliss. In *Purgatorio*, the foregrounding nears completion in Canto XXI with the appearance of Statius. He is a spirit bridge, a Latin poet and a Christian; his filial piety inclines backwards towards his beloved master, maker of the *Aeneid*, even as it leans, joyously, into imminent salvation and the City Of God. To have been a contemporary of Virgil, Statius avows, he would gladly spend another year on the mount of Purgatory. But only the one year. Canon is canon. Bliss is elsewhere. Yet, one love bridges both. And it is this love that impels the journey only perfect love can end. At the close of Canto XXI, in a moment of sublime tenderness *and* rigor, canon discloses its limits and also the final virtue of imperfection. Statius bows down to kiss his master's feet—

> But Virgil told him: "Brother, there's no need—
> you are a shade, a shade is what you see."
>   And rising, he: "Now you can understand
> how much burns in me for you, when I
> forget our insubstantiality,
>   Treating the shades as one treats solid things."
> (Mandelbaum, II. 130–36)

The "great teachers" (Statius and Virgil) keep, for one last time, the vigil of precedent. Statius is silent. Canon has no foresight beyond the speech and gestures by which it knows itself. What Dante is about to experience is wisdom freed from inwardness:

Vision plain. Virgil's has been a reflected light, a reflective wisdom. His guidance has only a farewell to say, in accents of abdication. Words give place to Word and lights to Light.

> . . .from now on, let your pleasure be your guide;
> you're past the steep and past the narrow paths.
>   Look at the sun that shines upon your brow;
> look at the grasses, flowers, and the shrubs
> born here, spontaneously, of the earth.
>   Among them, you can rest or walk until
> the coming of the glad and lovely eyes—
> those eyes that, weeping, sent me to your side.
>   Await no further word or sign from me . . .
>   (Mandelbaum, II. 131–39)

Ratio abdicates in favor of pleasure. The sole imperative is "Look." Summoned to a greater leisure in the garden where to rest and to walk articulate a single, inviolable pause (i.e., Eden), Dante becomes all eyes in sight of "the glad and lovely eyes" of his eventual Beatrice. Her word will be her name, not a text. Her image will be a sight, not a sign. Where the poets leave off, continuity foresees rest and motion united. The farther poem engrosses just this measureless singularity.

Yet, for the moment, singularity is a solitude unspeakably intense, albeit pregnant with reunion. In my present state of mind, I feel it exactly so. Any poem I currently imagine crowds itself into single words, isolated in their density and aching, not for the next word, but for the image of a name. I cannot say it. That task falls to a farther smile: "*Ben son, ben son Beatrice.*" Having made his translation of the opening tercets of *Purgatorio* XXVIII, Shelley transposed Dante's intensity into an agon of his own. As Richard Holmes explains, Shelley took "Matilda Gathering Flowers" and "developed it into the completed poem 'The Question,' with its ornate and exquisitely assembled description of a nosegay of 'visionary flowers'" (Holmes, 611). The flowers are sudden and unprecedented—"Bare Winter was suddenly changed to Spring"("The Question" 2)—as sudden, surely, as Virgil's silence and then Matilda's wordless song were to Dante. The flowers are, Shelley declares, "visionary"—as visionary, say, as those in Eliot's "Little Gidding": "a bloom more sudden / Than that of summer, neither budding nor fading, / Not in the scheme of generation." Yet, lacking the image of the eventual paradisal name, the plain utterance of which explains everything, the flowers embody only isolation and then the ache of it. Shelley concludes:

> Methought that of these visionary flowers
> I made a nosegay, bound in such a way
> That the same hues, which in their natural bowers
> Were mingled or opposed, the like array
> Kept these imprisoned children of the Hours
> Within my hand, and then, elate and gay,
> I hastened to the spot whence I had come,
> That I might there present it! Oh! to whom? (33-40)

There is no present without a name, and the name is not yet. Canon ends in a question canons cannot answer. Or perhaps I should say that canon's is not the answer for which, in a pause without dimension, my poetry aches.

In Denise Levertov's early poem, "The Ache of Marriage," there is a passage I've had in mind nearly every day for the past forty years and more: "two by two in the ark of / the ache of it" (12-13). It occurs to me now that Levertov, early and alone of the poets in my life, anticipates the location and nearly wordless threshold circumstance inside of which I write this. The passage indicates an enclosed space, an "ark" of certain but as yet featureless covenant. Marriage, like the finale I feel, is a canon of no text, an empty enclosure leaning forward, a discontinuity promising to be a singular and everlasting continuum. Marriage, like the finale I feel, breaks with the past on behalf of outcome. At the end of canon comes a break that is canon's true posterity. Virgil speaks no more. So, to begin, at last I come to *Purgatorio* XXVIII. The opening, in both the Mandelbaum and Shelley translations cited above, signals a wholly new and different line. Time is tempered to a slower motion, a stillness ambient and overwhelmed by sense and pleasure. Stevens had it wrong in "Sunday Morning." There *is* a "change of death in paradise." The change, however, is in itself intensely changeless. (A phrase from Keats's "Ode on a Grecian Urn" comes keenly to mind: "Pipe to the spirit ditties of no tone." [14]) The lines of poetry I want any more are slow, dense with fragrance and significance and aspects of eternity aching to marry each word to the next in unforeseeable reunion. The lines, like Dante's first motions of Eden, would cover the ark of a featureless covenant. Their music would sustain a pageantry time out of mind.

NaNMy state of mind is all the mind I have. As Rousseau opined near the end of his life, in *Reveries of a Solitary Walker*, "my ideas are nothing but sensations now." And it is, albeit briefly unaware, as a new-crowned solitary Dante steps towards Eden in *Purgatorio* XXVIII. All around him, new sensations crowd their meanings upon a mind made all of sense. (Exactly as words might crowd the lines of poetry I'm hoping still to write.) It is a morning mind, datum upon datum of joys.

> . . . birds welcomed those
> first hours of the morning joyously,
> and leaves supplied the burden to their rhymes—
>   (Mandelbaum, II.18–19)

Meaning is here indistinguishable from location and circumstance—which is to say that the burden of meaning is no burden. The branching lines support whispering leaves and the singing birds too. Green with it all, the branches mean exactly *as* they are. In such a state, in such a mind, all words rhyme. I look forward to poems of such a moment. A density that is no burden would be a continuing leisure, ambient and all-inclusive.

> Now, though my steps were slow, I'd gone so far
> Into the ancient forest that I could
> No longer see where I had made my entry.
>   (Mandelbaum, II.22–24)

Dante's early pleasures in the earthly paradise comprehend a limit and leave-taking of canon. The poet finds himself in a grove older than Time and illumined. Eden is not the *selva oscura* where his pilgrimage began. Showing no point of entry, here is a place made wholly of entrances and original permissions. Means of arrival (other poets, other poems) simply do not signify. From this point on, mere being is a present statement, fixed and expansive: lines stretching to eternity.

Slow as they are (a pace, a measure as appropriate to intensity as to leisure), the poet's steps take him to a river's edge. On the near shore of Lethe, Dante expounds a double vision. And he does so merely by standing where he stands. At the waters of Lethe, forgetfulness and self-knowledge are one and the same. Purification and transgression are one and the same. Immersion models ascension. Cleansed of remembrance, memory becomes original once again. This double vision is everything I want for any future lines of poetry. I want them cleanly, undistracted in their entirety. Only then, in full accord with the *via negativa* of the Classicist, might they bear witness to transcendence: a pause without dimensions. And I want them imaged to the allusive intensity of numberless flowers. Only then, in happy accord with the *via affirmativa* of the Romantic, will they delight in immanence: a garden never sown.

> All of the purest waters here on earth,
> when matched against that stream, would seem to be
> touched by impurity; it hides no thing—
> that stream—although it moves, dark, dark, beneath
> the never-ending shadows . . .
>
> (Mandelbaum, II.28–32)

In a darkness where nothing is hidden, in a motion fixed upon the margins of Eden, canon makes no argument. And without argument, canon is a solitary text. Reconciled, austerity and plentiful energy constitute a peerless singularity. Here is a strong-lined river at the edge of an ending.

It begins. Upon the far side of the river, strong in measure (the unintelligible sweetness of her song), dense in motif (the numberless flowers at her feet and in her arms), Matilda glides into view. Let us have Shelley's version. He is bold to emphasize the giddy sensorium that sparkles at canon's end.

... even as a thing
That suddenly, for a blank astonishment,
Charms every sense, and makes all thought take wing—
    A solitary woman! And she went
Singing and gathering flower after flower,
With which her way was painted and besprent.

(Shelley, II.37–42)

Dante is a blank of present statement—a blank all suddenly inscribed with sense. He occupies a ground not of thought, but of attention. Upon the departure of thought (and I honor Shelley for parsing it this way), exclamation takes the living form of singularity and vision: "A solitary woman!" Here is a Beatrice immediately prior to Beatrice. She is not a "screen lady" as was the woman in the *Vita Nuova*. Rather, she is the vivid precondition of a further poetry, audible just the other side of Lethe. It is art ("painted") and abundance ("besprent"), which is to say "pageant," that genre that succeeds canon by proving sufficient unto itself. Beauty knows its own. Virgil explained. Matilda embodies. Virgil led. Matilda summons. One step into the waters of forgetfulness and the future life of memory is assured. (*"Dove sta memora*," as Cavalcanti would have it.) Dante's present statement—joy without comprehension, fulfillment without possession—articulates the locus of his dearest wish: that seeing might interleave the volume of belief with loves. Flowers are the brackets and ground of his wish, and in Eden, the Purgatory's earthly paradise, they are crowns of forgetfulness and of the dense motifs, poems without pretext.

Shelley breaks off at just the moment when Matilda turns her face towards Dante. Her gesture gives immediate and entire pleasure. The music becomes articulate. *Fioretti* show their simple colors.

so did she turn, upon the little red
and yellow flowers, to me, no differently
that would a virgin, lowering her chaste eyes.
I had beseeched, and I was satisfied,
For she approached so close that the sweet sound
That reached me then became intelligible.

(Mandelbaum, II.55–60)

There is more to this turn than a simple *verso*. So very few steps away from canon, Dante already comes face to face with meaning of a new sort and instance. Eden's primitive is prime. The transformations accomplished by Matilda's turn are spontaneous, not sequential: suddenly reds and yellows; suddenly intelligible song. What elsewhere might require a ritual and rhetoric, acknowledgements and decorum, here springs forth in singular gesture. Cause and effect, beseeching and satisfaction breathe unitary being. Hue and melody blazon the sense of color and song, and Dante understands them. This is more than the Symbolists' dream of pure poetry. Theirs was an idea without a concept, an occult. For my part, and in the name of happiness, I want a poetry gotten of lines prior and subsequent to purity, something prime. Its durations would signify the instance of its meanings. Its density would be self-evident, not opaque, but imaged as a leisure continuing *with* as well as *into* the next lines. Lethe promises no less.

At the end of canon, Eden shows a panoramic smile, siting an epoch upon duration. Its primitive—a first age, a first utterance—profuses inward as the garden, becoming a surround. Matilda begins:

> "You are new here and may—because I smile
> in this place, chosen to be mankind's nest—
> wonder, perplexed, unable to detect
> the cause . . ."
>
> (Mandelbaum, II.77–80)

Dante's perplexity, as we shall see, is soon relieved. For the moment, he simply cannot understand how it is that, in Eden, breeze and freshet arise without apparent purposes or cause. Earlier in the poem, Statius (for "Statius" read "canon") had explained to Dante that no changes of weather were possible beyond the entrance to Purgatory. But canon cannot compass origin. It hasn't the syntax. In Canto XXVIII, climate proves to be indwelling, and indwelling confounds sequential tradition. The garden flourishes *within* a cause. The courses of air and water change *within* the changeless purpose: "this place, chosen to be mankind's nest." Matilda explains a nature that is new to

Dante, an atmosphere "within a circle, moved by the first circling" (1.104), and thus originary prior *and* subsequent to any shock of the New. It is almost as though Prospero and Miranda had exchanged advantages. The bittersweet irony of Shakespeare's magus ("'Tis new to thee") disappears when Miranda's "O brave new world" rings true. And the *Commedia* allows for no denying Matilda's truth. I like to anticipate, as any likely new line of mine, such a nest as this, where Matilda gathers flowers. She says:

> If what I've said were known, you would not need
> to be amazed on earth when growing things
> take root but have no seed that can be seen.
>   (Mandelbaum, II.115–17)

The newness of such a line would be supple and self-evident. It would be strong to avow the changes of the lines around it, rooted with them, but neither seeded nor seeding. It would forego that syntax, being (to take a phrase from Ashbery's "Some Trees," a poem beginning "These are amazing") distinctly one amidst a "chorus of smiles."

Edenic nature, as Matilda explains, is the inexhaustible fullness of an each and of an every: "the holy plain . . . is full of every seed" (II.118–19). Difference self-replicates, and so a changeless originality sustains variety, remains prolific, all the while fixed within its garden state. The pure products of the place "cannot be gathered;" their proper use is wholly reserved in evidence. And here my wish for poetry comes in sight of home. Lines various but inwardly profused; original statements whose meanings extend not into rhetoric but into the continuing evidence of themselves in concert. Articulateness without the gather-some burden of explanation. George Herbert once forecast, "The land of spices; something understood" ("Prayer I " 14). Hart Crane recollected momently from a future he could not span, "Whispers antiphonal in azure swing" ("Atlantis" 96). Such lines neither seek nor constitute a canon. They might, however, anticipate an afterlife, a pause articulated upon the land to which we go. Of each, it may be said, as Matilda says of the rivers of Eden,

it issues from a pure and changeless fountain,
which by the will of God regains as much
as, on two sides, it pours and it divides.

(Mandelbaum, II. 124–26)

"My word I poured," Hart Crane avowed in his last poem "The Broken Tower." The line I have in mind divides without diminishing. Neither is it emptied into stanza or paraphrase. It ends and never fails.

The waters are twinned in Eden, distinct but inseparable both in purpose and in proof. To my mind, they are clear lines ("pure and changeless") in a flawless passage. Sure enough, Dante's passage over the twin rivers Lethe and Eunoe marks the path of perfection: early steps beyond the earthly paradise towards Paradise itself. Bathed in forgetfulness, Dante remembers his and everyone's original souls, born adepts of Eden. Crossing Eunoe then, and bathed there in memory of the Good (*dove sta memora*), original being is competent to affirm the intensity and continuity of Heaven's leisure. Here I am bound to cite a dictum of Geoffrey Hill's: "if we are to allow 'intensity,' we must also press for 'density'" ("A Postscript on Modernist Poetics," 572). Is it wrong to imagine—which is to say "image"—perfection? It is hapless to imagine thus in adumbration of eternity, "Whispers antiphonal in azure swing?" If there is still another poem of mine to make, I see it dense with affirmation. The first caesura comprises a forgetting, and the next one gladly recalls imagery setting a task. Every line is the axis of a smile, every stanza the broad and easy way from negation to "the land of spices; something understood."

States of mind are inexplicable, but given world enough (our books are worlds, as we learned in childhood) and given words that flaunt their inwardness like emblems, they flower. Canons end in the continuity they cannot compass. That is their happiness.

Then I turned round completely, and I faced
my poets; I could see that they had heard
with smiles this final corollary spoken;
that done, my eyes returned to the fair woman.

(Mandelbaum, II. 145–48)

Purgatorio XXVIII ends beyond any words of Statius' or of Virgil's, and the poets are glad. Their company, their guidance, sound and sense show a valedictory smile. Dante turns away from all that, returning to origin. The further *Commedia* is pageantry. I love to learn it. Haste vanishes in rapture. The intensity of nothing more to say becomes immensity.

In memory of Geoffrey Hill

Coda

Whenever I gaze on Waterloo sunset
I am in paradise.

—Ray Davies

Desire vanishes into duration. That is Paradise. The magic of a gaze turns inside out, surrounding the eye with a sudden Eden, a comprehensive instance unaccountable, by all accounts ("and the darkness comprehended it not"). Waterloo sunset . . . or, if you wake early with William Blake, the sun rising at Felpham, "as an Innumerable company of the Heavenly host" (*Vision of the Last Judgement* 44). Unaccountable or innumerable, whichever you prefer, the measures are Edenic. And the measurement of Paradise begins in gaze, ending only when the lost word (Eden) is reinvented and the attentions lapse. I never forget the confounded innocence of Hart Crane's "Voyages II" finally exhausted in "The seal's wide spindrift gaze toward paradise" (25). Originally, Crane had not written "wide spindrift" but, rather, "findrinny." The publishers wouldn't hear of it; the awkward, onomatopoeic word appeared in none of their dictionaries. So, Crane revised, and paradise drifted away. Years after Crane's death, the scholars resurrected "findrinny" from the wreck of Ahab's *Pequod*. But they were too late. (For the whole story, see Malcolm Cowley's classic *Exile's Return*.) The lost word was reinvented, and the attentions lapsed.

It's happened to me. Not often, nor even seldom perhaps, but sometimes the vastation of a moment has imparadised me. Desire—for rest, for happiness, for a poem—has dis-

appeared into the duration of an ample, sudden light all unprepared but absolute. All that was required of me was gaze.
The first time it happened I was in the family car in a woodland, and I've done my best to describe it in an earlier essay,
"Wine instead of Whiskey for a While." It happened again in
the Cloisters museum, in the north of Manhattan. As a teen-
ager, I'd taken to spending my birthdays there, always finish-
ing the day in a little fountain close, the Trie Cloister. And it
was in the Trie I wrote nearly all of my first haphazard poems,
usually on the fly-leaf of whatever book I'd brought to read.
On one particular birthday, a Sunday, I was gladly all alone
beside the fountain, and the splash of water on the stonework
sounded like sunlight. A door opened. A little girl with nobody beside her, in her first communion dress, walked toward
the fountain and played her fingertips across the water. The
sunlight amplified. The white of her communion dress became
blinding, though I was not blinded. The water paused, entirely possessed. For the moment, eternity was at rest in real time.
The child disappeared. The light remained.

Not all that long ago, I was out walking in the high
country near the edge of Utah's Little Cottonwood Canyon.
I had no destination in mind, only time to fill at the end of
a day of academic rigmarole at a hotel below. Nothing could
have been further from my mind than poetry or Paradise. The
woods deepened and the ground inclined more sharply. Twi-
light fell sooner than I'd expected, and I lost the path. But I
felt no anxiety at all in what normally, for me, would have been
a very anxious situation. I'm no woodsman. And then, a few
yards to my front, a length of fallen deadwood began to glow.
The trees around me brightened, nearly to whiteness. Whiter
still, the path before me shone clear. I didn't move. There was
no reason to move, no point in hurrying. I saw no visible limit
to the light and felt no motion in the air. The path was not a vi-
tal route to safety, as I'd supposed. It was a point of rest. I rest-
ed. Then I was back at the hotel.

I've stumbled upon, or into, some few other sudden
Edens in my life. But all too often, loving friends have sought
to assure me that each, in its way, had been a dream. I have nev-

er found words to explain how absolutely certain I am that I was not dreaming, that I have been to Paradise awake and alive. Like many of my generation, my earliest model of a poet in the contemporary world was Dylan Thomas—the orotund, vocable, tirelessly articulate ambassador of Eden as Eden shines clear in "Fern Hill," "Under Milk Wood," and "In Country Sleep." And all my writing life, I've been haunted and worried by something he said at the catastrophic end of *his* life: "May my children forgive me. I want to die and to go to Heaven." What I have to say, what I have always wanted to say, is this: "I've been to Heaven alive and well." If I'm wrong, then, as far as I'm concerned, the universe is a sorry mismatch between vanity and wishful thinking. In my poems, I do not speak of dreams, as in the great dream visions of Chaucer and Guillaume de Lorris. I do not speak in allegory, as does Spenser in the Garden of Adonis. I do not speak of nascent memory, as do Traherne in "Wonder" and Wordsworth in the "Ode: Intimations of Immortality." I speak of the sudden, unearned and certainly unprepared perfection of attention I can only describe as "gaze."

There are precedents. Exalted far beyond the scope of my own haphazard, there are, nevertheless, precedents. I think of Dante taken unawares by the Earthly Paradise, the garden subsequent to Eden in which he is, at last, given to lift his eyes into the eyes of Beatrice. The sole imperative, once again, is to gaze. The maiden Virtues accompanying Beatrice command: "*Fa che le viste non risparmi*" ("Be not sparing of your gaze"). I think of the prolonged vastation of Ezra Pound's *Rock-Drill de los Cantares*, the duration in which a child may "walk in peace in her basilica, / The light there almost solid" ("Canto XCIII" 177-178), Pound's motto and motive of this is taken from Richard of St. Victor on the subject of gaze: *Ubi amor, ibi oculus est* ("Where love is, there is the eye"). And, too, I think of D.H. Lawrence at the end of his life, venturing everything upon a gaze:

> The gods are nameless and imageless
> yet looking in a great full lime-tree of summer
> I suddenly saw deep into the eye of god:
> It is enough.
>
> ("What Are the Gods," 2-5)

I've been to Heaven alive. I'm unprepared but hoping to return. Because it's easy, and because I have no choice, I'm willing to trust that something avowed by Yeats in his *Autobiography* is entirely true: "He (God) asks nothing but attention" (318).

Works Cited

Alcott, Bronson. *Conversations with Children on the Gospels*, Lindisfarne, 1991.

Alighieri, Dante. *Purgatorio*, translated by Allen Mandelbaum, U of California P, 1981.

Arnold, Matthew. *Selected Poems and Prose*, J.M. Dent, 1993.

Artaud, Antonin. "Electroshock Fragments," *Artaud Anthology*, edited by Jack Hirschman, City Lights Books, 1965, 183-90.

Ashbery, John. "As One Put Drunk into the Packet-Boat," *Collected Poems 1956-1987*, edited by Mark Ford, Library of America, 2008, 427-428.

___. "Self-Portrait in a Convex Mirror," ibid., 474-487.

___. "Soonest Mended," ibid., 184-186.

___. "Syringa," ibid., 534-536.

___. "The New Spirit," ibid. 247-280.

___. "The Picture of Little J.A. in a Prospect of Flowers," ibid., 13-14.

___. "Vaucanson," ibid., 830-831.

Barnard, John, ed. *John Keats: The Complete Poems*, Penguin 1973.

Barnard, Mary. *Sappho*, University of California Press, 2012.

Beckett, Samuel. *Three Novels (Molloy, Malone Dies, The Unnamable).* Grove Press, 1959.

___. *Stories & Texts for Nothing*, Grove Press, 1967.

Blake, William, "The Marriage of Heaven and Hell," *The Oxford Authors: William Blake*, edited by Michael Mason, Oxford UP, 1988, 8-20.

___. "Vision of the Last Judgement," ibid., 35-45.

___. "Visions of the Daughters of Albion," ibid. 196-202.

Brooke, Rupert. "Dining Room Tea," *The Collected Poems of Rupert Brooke*, Dodd, Mead & Co., 1923, 90-92.

___. "Peace," ibid., 107.

Brooks, Cleanth, ed. *Complete Poetry and Selected Prose of John Milton*, Random House, 1950.

Caws, Mary Ann, ed. *Mallarme in Prose*, New Directions, 2001.

Celan, Paul. "Cello Entry," *Poems of Paul Celan*, edited and translated by Michael Hamburger, Persea Books, 1988, 253.

___. "How You," ibid. 297.

Ceravolo, Joseph. *The Green Lake Is Awake*, Coffee House Press, 1994.

Crane, Hart. "Chaplinesque," *Hart Crane: Complete Poems and Selected Letters*, edited by Langdon Hammer, Library of America, 2006, 9.

___. "Tenderness and Resolution," ibid., 136.

___. "The Mango Tree," ibid. 79-80.

Creeley, Robert. *Autobiography*, Hanuman Books, 1991.

___. "I Know a Man," *The Collected Poems of Robert Creeley 1945-1975*, U of California P, 1982, 132.

___. "The Warning," ibid. 140.

___. *If I Were Writing This*, New Directions, 2003.

___. *On Earth*, U of California P, 2006.

Duncan, Robert. *Selected Poems*, New Directions, 1993.

Eliot, T. S. *The Complete Poems and Plays*. New York, Harcourt, 1952.

Guest, Barbara. "Noisetone," *The Collected Poems of Barbara Guest*, edited by Hadley Haden Guest, Wesleyan UP, 2008, 471.

___. "Red Lilies," ibid., 99.

___. "Roses," ibid., 128-29.

___. "The Location of Things," ibid. 3-4.

Hass, Robert. "Against Botticelli" in *Praise*, The Ecco Press, 1979, 10-12.

___. "Meditation at Lagunitas," ibid. 4-5.

Herbert, George. *The Temple*, edited by Louis Martz. Oxford UP, 1986.

Hill, Geoffrey. *The Lords of Limit*, Oxford UP, 1985.

Hillman, Brenda. *Fortress*. Wesleyan UP, 1989.

Holmes, Richard. *Shelley: The Pursuit*, E.P. Dutton & Co., 1975.

Howard, Richard. *Fellow Feelings*, Athenaeum, 1976.

Jabes, Edmond. *El, or the Last Book,* translated by Rosmarie Waldrop, Wesleyan UP, 1991.

Jensen, Laura. *Memory*, Dragon Gate Inc., 1982.

Joyce, James. *Finnegans Wake*, Viking Press, 1959.

Kermode, Frank, and Joan Richardson eds. *Wallace Stevens: Collected Poetry and Prose*, Library of America, 1997.

Levertov, Denise. *O Taste and See*, New Directions, 1964.

Larbaud, Valery. "Ode," translated by William Jay Smith, *The Random House Book of Twentieth-Century French Poetry*, edited by Paul Auster, Random House, 1982.

Lauterbach, Ann. *Clamor*, Viking Penguin, 1991.

Lawrence, D.H. *Last Poems*, Heinemann, 1932.

Lowell, Robert. *For the Union Dead*, Farrar, Straus & Giroux, 1964.

Mallarmé, Stéphane. *A Tomb for Anatole*, translated by Paul Auster, North Point Press, 1983.

McEwan, Ian. *Saturday*. Jonathan Cape, 2005.

Mason, Wyatt ed. *The Letters of Arthur Rimbaud, Volume II*, Modern Library, 2003.

Merwin, W. S. *The Carrier of Ladders*, Athenaeum, 1970.

Miller, Henry. *The Time of the Assassins*, New Directions, 1962.

Nabokov, Vladimir. *Lolita*, Putnam, 1958.

O'Hara, Frank. "Joseph Cornell," *The Collected Poems of Frank O'Hara*, edited by Donald Allen, U of California P, 1995, 237.

___. "Meditations in an Emergency," ibid., 197-98.

Plomer, William ed. *Kilvert's Diary*, Pimlico, 1999.

Pound, Ezra. "LXXVI," *The Cantos of Ezra Pound,* New Directions, 1996, 472-83.

___. "XCII," ibid., 638-42.

___. "Notes for CXVII et seq.," ibid., 821-23.

Ramke, Bin. *The Erotic Light of Gardens*, Wesleyan UP, 1989.

Read, Bill. *The Days of Dylan Thomas*, McGraw-Hill, 1964.

Revell, Donald. "For Thomas Traherne," *Pennyweight Windows: New & Selected Poems*, Alice James Books, 2005, 170.

___. "How Passion Comes to Matter," ibid., 37-38.

Rimbaud, Arthur. "Bad Blood," *A Season in Hell*, translated by
Donald Revell, Omnidawn, 2007, 23-35.
___. "Deliriums II," ibid. 53-65.
___. "Farewell," ibid., 77-79.
___. "Morning," ibid. 75.
___. "O Seasons, O Chateaux," ibid., 65.
___. "The Impossible," ibid., 67-71.
Roe, Nicholas ed. *William Wordsworth: Selected Poetry*, Penguin, 1992.
Rousseau, Jean-Jacques. *Reveries of the Solitary Walker*. Translated
by Peter France, London, Penguin, 1974.
Sayre, Robert F. ed. *Henry David Thoreau: A Week, Walden, The Maine
Woods, Cape Cod*, Library of America, 1985.
Schuyler, James. "A Few Days," *Collected Poems*, Farrar, Straus &
Giroux, 1993, 354-79.
___. "Autumn Leaves," ibid., 324-25.
___. "Dear Joe," ibid., 318-19.
___. "Lilacs," ibid., 310-11.
___. "Moon," ibid., 321.
___. "O Sleepless Night," ibid., 339-45.
___. "The Rose of Marion," ibid., 307-08.
___. "An Interview with Mark Hillringhouse," *American Poetry Re-
view*, Volume 14, number 2, March/April 1985, 5-12.
Shelley, Percy Bysshe. "Matilda Gathering Flowers," *The Com-
plete Poetical Works*, Houghton Mifflin, 1901, 523-24.
___. "The Question," ibid. 389-90.
Stevenson, W.H. *William Blake*, Penguin, 1988.
Stratford, Philip ed. *The Portable Graham Greene*, The Viking
Press, 1973.
Thomas, Dylan. *Collected Poems*, New Directions, 1953.
Traherne, Thomas. "Centuries of Meditation: The Fourth
Century," *Thomas Traherne: Poems, Centuries and Three Thanksgiv-
ings*, edited by Ann Ridler, Oxford UP, 1966, 316-66.
___. "Ease," ibid., 35-36.
___. "Eden," ibid., 8-10.
___. "Felicity," ibid., 81.
___. "Innocence," ibid., 10-12.
___. "The Anticipation," ibid. 52-56.
___. "The Apostasy," ibid., 86-88.

___. "The Preparative," ibid., 12-14.

___. "The Vision," ibid., 15-17.

___. "Wonder," ibid., 6-8.

Twain, Mark. *The Adventures of Huckleberry Finn*, Vintage, 2010.

Valery, Paul. "Literature," *Selected Writings of Paul Valery*, New Directions, 1950, 147-52.

___. "On Mallarme," ibid., 213-21.

___. "The Memories of a Poem," ibid., 159-61.

Vuillard, Edouard. *Foliage-Oak Tree and Fruit Seller*. 1918, The Art Institute of Chicago.

Williams, William Carlos. "Spring and All XVIII," *Imaginations*, New Directions, 1970, 133.

___. "The rose is obsolete," ibid., 107-08.

___. *Paterson*, New Directions, 1948.

Wood, Susan. *Bazaar*, Holt, Rinehart and Winston, 1981.

W.B. Yeats. *The Autobiography of William Butler Yeats*, Macmillan, 1953.

About the Author

Donald Revell is the author of fifteen collections of poetry, most recently of *The English Boat* (2018) and *Drought-Adapted Vine* (2015), both from Alice James books, Revell has also published six volumes of translations from the French, including Apollinaire's *Alcools*, Rimbaud's *A Season in Hell*, Laforgue's *Last Poems*, and Verlaine's *Songs without Words*. His critical writings have been collected as *Essay: A Critical Memoir*; *The Art of Attention*; and *Invisible Green: Selected Prose*. Winner of the PEN USA Translation Award and two-time winner of the PEN USA Award for Poetry, he has also won The Academy of American Poets' Lenore Marshall Prize and is a former Fellow of the Ingram Merrill and Guggenheim Foundations. Additionally, he has been twice awarded Fellowships from the National Endowment for the Arts. Having previously taught at the universities of Alabama, Denver, Iowa, Missouri, Tennessee and Utah, Donald Revell is currently Professor of English at the University of Nevada, Las Vegas.

Photograph of the author by
Jeffrey Peters. Used by permission.